Masculinities in Post-Millennial Popular Romance

This book focuses on the projection of the hero's masculinity in a selection of post-millennial popular romance narratives and attempts to discover if, and to what extent, this projection reinforces or challenges patriarchal ideas about gender. In the majority of these narratives the hero is often presented as a hegemonic alpha male. However, hegemonic masculinity is not a fixed concept. Rather, it is subject to continuous change which allows for the emergence of various dominant masculinities. Under a poststructuralist lens and through a close textual analysis approach and a gender reading of romance narratives, the book suggests that to a certain extent the romance hero could be described as a platform onto which different forms of dominant masculinity are displayed and highlights that these masculinities do not necessarily clash, depend on, or function as a prerequisite for each other.

Eirini Arvanitaki is a teaching associate in the Department of Social Sciences at the Hellenic Open University in Patras, Greece.

Routledge Focus on Literature

Neurocognitive Interpretations of Australian Literature
Criticism in the Age of Neuroawareness
Jean-François Vernay

Mapping the Origins of Figurative Language in Comparative Literature
Richard Trim

Metaphors of Mental Illness in Graphic Medicine
Sweetha Saji and Sathyaraj Venkatesan

Wanderers
Literature, Culture and the Open Road
David Brown Morris

Sham Ruins
A User's Guide
Brian Willems

The New Midlife Self-Writing
Emily O. Wittman

Female Physicians in American Literature
Abortion in 19th-Century Literature and Culture
Margaret Jay Jessee

Masculinities in Post-Millennial Popular Romance
Eirini Arvanitaki

For more information about this series, please visit: www.routledge.com/Routledge-Focus-on-Literature/book-series/RFLT

Masculinities in Post-Millennial Popular Romance

Eirini Arvanitaki

NEW YORK AND LONDON

First published 2022
by Routledge
605 Third Avenue, New York, NY 10158

and by Routledge
4 Park Square, Milton Park, Abingdon, Oxon, OX14 4RN

Routledge is an imprint of the Taylor & Francis Group, an informa business

© 2022 Eirini Arvanitaki

The right of Eirini Arvanitaki to be identified as author of this work has been asserted in accordance with sections 77 and 78 of the Copyright, Designs and Patents Act 1988.

All rights reserved. No part of this book may be reprinted or reproduced or utilised in any form or by any electronic, mechanical, or other means, now known or hereafter invented, including photocopying and recording, or in any information storage or retrieval system, without permission in writing from the publishers.

Trademark notice: Product or corporate names may be trademarks or registered trademarks, and are used only for identification and explanation without intent to infringe.

Library of Congress Cataloging-in-Publication Data
Names: Arvanitaki, Erini, author.
Title: Masculinities in post-millennial popular romance / Erini Arvanitaki.
Description: New York, NY : Routledge, 2022. | Series: Routledge focus on literature ; 01 | Includes bibliographical references and index.
Identifiers: LCCN 2022003707 (print) | LCCN 2022003708 (ebook) | ISBN 9781032065656 (hardback) | ISBN 9781032306841 (paperback) | ISBN 9781003202837 (ebook)
Subjects: LCSH: Romance fiction—History and criticism. | Masculinity in literature. | Men in literature. | Heroes in literature. | Sex role in literature. | Popular literature—21st century—History and criticism.
Classification: LCC PN3448.L67 A78 2022 (print) | LCC PN3448. L67 (ebook) | DDC 809.3/85—dc23/eng/20220211
LC record available at https://lccn.loc.gov/2022003707
LC ebook record available at https://lccn.loc.gov/2022003708

ISBN: 978-1-032-06565-6 (hbk)
ISBN: 978-1-032-30684-1 (pbk)
ISBN: 978-1-003-20283-7 (ebk)

DOI: 10.4324/9781003202837

Typeset in Times New Roman
by Apex CoVantage, LLC

To Michael and our two bundles of joy

Contents

Acknowledgements   viii

Introduction   1

1   Hegemonic Masculinity and the Romance Hero   17

2   Transnational Business Masculinities in Popular Romance Fiction   25

    Press and Fame   31
    Cosmopolitanism and Attachment to Place   36

3   Hybrid Masculine Bloc in Popular Romance Fiction   43

    Emotional (In)accessibility   43
    Self-restraint   47

4   Body and Beauty in Popular Romance Fiction   53

5   "Lesser" Masculinities   60

6   Conclusion   64

Index   67

Acknowledgements

This book has been one of my greatest achievements so far. There were times when it seemed like an unattainable goal, a task well beyond my abilities, and it would have never been possible without certain notable people whom I hold dear. For this reason, I would like to thank those who believed in me and supported me.

There are no words that can express the debt of gratitude I owe to Michael who spent countless hours babysitting our little ones, G. and O., so that I can have the opportunity to concentrate and finish this project on time. For looking after me, taking care of me, keeping me sane, and helping me keep the balance between work and family – you are my hero.

A very special thank you goes to my parents O. and E. for helping out in any way possible from the very beginning to the completion of this book. You never doubted my abilities.

A great and heartfelt thank you to Mr Campbell McPherson whose comments and advice on earlier drafts of the book helped pave the way forward. I am truly grateful and honoured to call you friend.

A big thank you to Professor Catherine Belsey and Professor Deborah Philips who looked at earlier drafts of this work with a critical eye, provided support, and encouraged me to publish my work.

This book is dedicated to all of you, thank you.

Introduction

Romance has incrementally grown in popularity over the past century. The first Mills & Boon romance novel was published in 1909[1] and since then romance has not only survived but also become a long-standing genre. There are several reasons behind its durability and success. First, its ability to please and appeal to a mass audience. For Pierre Bourdieu, romance novels are products of "worldly or *commercial success*" (1996: 218) situated in "the field of large-scale production"[2] (1993: 125), especially if one takes into account the high volume of romance novels published, translated, and distributed all around the world every month.[3] According to Bourdieu, the continuous production of such narratives "arises from *demand*" (45). In a similar vein, Ken Gelder terms romance an "entertainment industry" because of its *highly* consumable nature and also due to its ability to engage and amuse the readers (2004: 51).

Second, what has also contributed to keeping the romance genre alive for so long is the content of the books and their effect on the reader. These are stories of two individuals who meet, fall in love, face obstacles, and successfully overcome them. Through the love plots, the books address anxieties, concerns, and everyday troubles that the average reader can identify with. Additionally, the romance novel is a means of escapism from everyday life and responsibilities as well as a short-lived opportunity to enjoy personal time/space and focus on one's self (Radway [1984] 1991: 61).

Third, the genre's ability to adapt to the periods and societies in which it is published has also assisted in prolonging its longevity. Scott McCracken postulates that "contemporary popular fiction" survives the continuous changes of our time by

> perform[ing] complex negotiations, mapping historical and spatial changes in a period of rapid globalisation, when local identities are being restructured in relation to an international culture. Popular fiction

DOI: 10.4324/9781003202837-1

draws on existing popular tropes, but is also engaged in mapping the experience of new social relations.

(2012: 119)

Or as Jan Cohn puts it, "The contemporary romance manages to trim and adjust aspects of the stories it tells so as to maintain a degree of up-to-dateness" (1988: 10–11).

As the dominant market leader in popular romance novels, the success of Harlequin, which owns imprint Mills & Boon, has not come without effort or creativity, especially with regard to its marketing strategies. According to Glen Thomas, the marketing strategy that Harlequin and Mills & Boon follow is typical for the creative industries (2012: 211–13), a conception which he borrows from John Hartley (2005: 6). A creative industry brings together the creative arts (culture) and the cultural industries (market). Harlequin and Mills & Boon is a company where "authors are thereby producers or creative workers who provide content for publishers. Publishers offer authors the means to distribute and market this creative product to the reader (or consumer)" (Thomas 2012: 211).

The company's rapid transformation to become the largest corporate producer of romance fiction is partly down to Lawrence Heisey (a former manager from Proctor and Gamble) and his innovative marketing methods. Heisey emphasised the idea that romances could be marketed as a brand rather than focusing on promoting individual authors (Grescoe 1996: 76). Establishing a brand identity was, and still is, of great significance to Harlequin and Mills & Boon. The American Marketing Association defines branding as "a name, term, sign, symbol, or design, or a combination of them, intended to identify the goods or services of one seller or a group of sellers and to differentiate them from those of competitors" (Kotler 2000: 188). Moreover, promoting books from different authors under a brand name constructs an image of romances as reliable products of a reputable quality, that is, "uniform, homogenized, quality controlled in the same way each bar of Ivory soap is quality controlled" (Dystel 1980: 22). Brands are important to both the company and its consumers (the readers, in this case) as they are "about defining expectations and then satisfying them" (Royle et al. 1999: 5). The Harlequin and Mills & Boon brand name "acts as a reassurance to the reader that the terms of that salacious property, Romance, will not vary" (Philips 1990: 101).

In addition, amongst Heisey's innovative methods for marketing romances were the free sampling of new novels, a change in the selling points of romances from bookstores to supermarkets and drugstores, the promotion of products in television advertisements and women's magazines (such as *Cosmopolitan*, *Glamour*, *Redbook*, and *Good Housekeeping*)

(Ireland et al. 2006: 162) and the establishment of Harlequin Reader Service[4] through which readers used to receive new titles (monthly by post) with more than 50% discount (Graves 2014: 3). John Markert also recognises these marketing techniques as the crux of the company's growth:

> [S]tandardization of content and the "fine-tuning" of distribution to select retail establishments was a major factor in Harlequin's success; it allowed (1) a more precise estimate of the number of books to be printed; (2) a clearer perception of the prospective consumer [. . .] and (3) introductory offers and advertising to focus more narrowly on the specific consumers most likely to enjoy Harlequin's product.
> (1985: 77)

Other techniques that contributed to the company being the "800-pound gorilla of the category" (Danford et al. 2003) were the following: first, the establishment of principal offices in "Amsterdam, Athens, Budapest, Hamburg, Granges-Paccot [Switzerland], London, Madrid, Milan, New York, Paris, Rio de Janeiro, Stockholm, Sydney, Tokyo, Toronto, and Warsaw" (McWilliam 2009: 4) and other smaller offices in "Malaysia, Singapore, Korea, the Philippines, Thailand and Eastern Europe" (Creed 2003: 100) which contributed to the global expansion of the company. In 2009, the publisher announced plans for further expansion in countries such as China and India (Andriani 2009). The penetration of international markets helped lower the cost of distribution as "separate publishing companies were set up overseas to publish directly in the indigenous language" (McAleer 1999: 284–5). With the opening of local offices came the introduction of series on other cultures such as the Indian Authors Collection, Harlequin Kimani Arabesque, and African-American. This marketing strategy indicates not only the company's attempt to build an international brand image but also their understanding of distinct local markets and the need to adapt to suit local reader's needs (i.e. think global act local). Yoram Wind (1986: 26) originally coined the term "think globally, act locally" (otherwise known as glocalisation) to refer to companies that standardise the features of their brand (e.g. logo, corporate identity, and slogans) but adapt to and localise certain elements of their products (e.g. content, packaging, place/distribution, price) to suit a particular country. Harlequin and Mills & Boon achieved this by adapting its products to target markets: "as far as editorial freedom is concerned, the local companies enjoy the freedom to make decisions that suit the local market" (Paizis 2006: 135). Its glocalisation strategy has involved standardising the brand but adapting to the content or covers of the novels.[5] Romances published and distributed in more conservative regions (e.g. Asia and the Middle East) are adjusted and tailored to include less sexual content and with tamer covers in an attempt to embrace cultural differences and not offend the moral attitudes of readers from these regions (Tapper 2014: 252). Another example of product adaptation to local markets is the repackaging of popular romances in Japan as "manga" (comic books with colourful covers) to attract and appeal to a young Japanese readership. This move was highly successful, with 18 million copies sold in 2003 (Bodsworth 2004).

The company has also adapted its distribution strategies (i.e. through libraries in the 1930s and 1940s) over the decades. For example, in the 1960s, novels were "given away in boxes of feminine napkins", as McAleer coyly puts it, and delivered by post "along with special gifts and questionnaires on [the readers'] tastes in reading" (McAleer 1999: 284–5; McWilliam 2009: 141). Similarly, the company was quick to respond to international political developments by distributing 750,000 novels to women from East Germany after the fall of the Berlin Wall in 1990, and the unfurling of a heart-shaped banner in Warsaw in 1992 on Valentine's Day (285). Like many other companies, Mills & Boon (in the UK) was equally quick to respond to the Polish migration wave to expand its readership and increase its sales. In 2004, Poland joined the European Union and since then over 230,000 Polish workers have moved to the UK in pursuit of employment. Four years later, Mills & Boon decided to translate a dozen of its titles into Polish and distributed them to stores (e.g. WHSmith) across the UK, particularly in regional areas with sizeable Polish populations. Claire Somerville, the sales and marketing director of Mills & Boon, explains why this is a great opportunity for Mills & Boon: "New immigrants are well catered for in terms of other products like food and newspapers, but nobody has quite moved into the book market yet. This is just to meet the changing face of our UK readership" (Borland 2008).

The company's rapid engagement with literary trends and fast-growing niche markets proved to be another strategic success as its approach was one "where producers deliver to consumers what consumers want, rather than what the producer *thinks* consumers want" (Thomas 2012: 213). Keeping up with such changing market trends, reading habits and increasing the number of readers were of great importance for the company. As the president and chief executive officer (CEO) of Harlequin, Donna Hayes noted, "We always want to keep our loyal fans happy [. . .] but we like to bring them something new, too" and "attracting new readers is always a focus at Harlequin" (Hayes in Danford et al. 2003). A further technique that Harlequin used was to expand into already-existing romance subcategories. For example, in September 1998, the company tapped into the niche market of Christian fiction and released its first three inspirational romances which celebrated traditional values (i.e. heart, home, and family) (Woodard 1998: 36). Moreover, in October 2003, Harlequin Flipside (the first romantic comedy series of Harlequin) made its first appearance (production has now been ceased). According to Hayes, the humour in this series was "edgier and more ironic, less dependent on physical comedy". A year later, the Silhouette Bombshell series was introduced. These were action/adventure stories that featured heroines presented as "tough, courageous and 100% guaranteed to blow you away" (Hayes cited in Danford et al. 2003). The paranormal trend evoked by the literary success of Stephenie Meyer's vampire-themed series (*Twilight, New Moon, Eclipse, Breaking Dawn*) – first volume published in 2005 – was the generating source for the creation of the Nocturne (exclusively in an eBook format) series for Harlequin and Mills & Boon in 2006 (Ramsdell 2012: 620).

Harlequin and Mills & Boon's focus on expanding its market base and profitability was reflected in 2008 when the company decided to diversify into the nonfiction market. One of the causes was the popularity of *Friends: A Love Story*[6] (130,000 copies in print) and the attention it received. Despite the company being known mostly for the publication of romance fiction, Harlequin and Mills & Boon in 2007 announced in *Publisher's Weekly* about the release of nonfiction books on sex, health, relationships, fitness, and love. Having acquired experience and knowledge on what women want, the publisher seemed confident that its line of nonfiction books would be a welcome addition (Milliot 2007). However, this strategic move to enter the nonfiction market did not require the creation of a new romance subcategory. Rather, these nonfiction works were published under already-established imprints such as Mira, Harlequin, and Steeple Hill.

In her article in *The Guardian*, Alison Flood makes suggests that a year after the appearance and immense success of *Fifty Shades of Grey* (which was published in 2011), Harlequin and Mills & Boon was quick to borrow from the successful trend of E.L. James's book and announced the circulation of its own erotica series (12 Shades of Surrender) which consisted of 12 short stories (only available as eBooks) (Flood 2012). That is not to say that novels with more explicit content were something new to the company as the Harlequin Desire series, as well as Silhouette's Sensation and Sensual Romance all predated James's book (these series were launched in 1983, 1988, and 2000, respectively).[7] Nevertheless, the reason behind the continuous expansion and also introduction of new subgenres of romance was to keep up with contemporary trends in the publishing market, product diversification, and the readers' interests. As Hayes put it, "[A]s long as women's interests and lives are changing we will reflect these changes in our books" (Hayes cited in Danford et al. 2003). This marketing strategy highlights the "customer-centric"[8] relationship of Harlequin and Mills & Boon with its readership. From its inception till the present day, the company places great emphasis on its readers and pays close attention to feedback received from them. Through the establishment of "a market-research department [the company] monitor[s] which of [its] various series [are] likely to appeal to which sectors and why". This valuable information is received – via organising public events such as "reader thank you parties" (Jensen 1984: 42), annual surveys, and online polls[9] – analysed, and fed back to the publishers. As a result, "[T]he books are shaped to appear at the right intervals and dates, to be of the best length, to carry the optimum information and have the most attractive design of the covers" (Paizis 2006: 130).

Moreover, and in line with the advancements in internet technology, in Sydney, in 1998, the company established an internet presence by launching its first website to provide readers with information regarding the company and its products while simultaneously adding another purchasing channel via e-commerce (i.e. their online website). On its website, a synopsis of each series and book is given along with pictures of their covers. The combination of written information and pictures helps encourage the readers to make an online purchase. A decade later, the Australian company launched the first digitalised series of novels (eBooks). Due to a growing demand for eBooks, Harlequin and Mills & Boon also released its own digital reading application for iPhone and iPad devices in 2011; however, this app is no longer available. In an article featured in *The Guardian*, Tim Cooper, Harlequin's digital and marketing director, states that the decision behind the launch of this application was taken with the readers' convenience, reading pace, and frequency in mind: "Digital lends itself to the habitual nature of our content. Our readers finish reading one and they can download the next" (Dredge 2014). Providing an e-commerce channel allows publishers to communicate with their customers directly and a lot quicker than other communication channels (e.g. over the phone or in store). Digital platforms (i.e. eBooks) also allow readers to have greater privacy in what they are reading and also if they dislike what they are reading they can almost instantaneously move onto another novel. The availability of alternative novels is made visible on Harlequin and Mills & Boon website to draw the readers' attention to similar novels. This technique also acts as a promotional deploy to further drive demand for its products and also gives greater choice to the readers. Reading books online also gives readers the opportunity to provide instant feedback seamlessly, or as Tapper notes, "the online proliferation of happy-ever-after blogs, review sites and online forums creates enormous marketing leverage to [romance] publishers – a natural advantage traditional publishers are struggling to duplicate" (2014: 256).

The move towards providing eBooks is another example of product differentiation and has been applauded by readers as it gives them an unashamed literary freedom and removes the feeling of embarrassment they may experience when seen with a romance novel in hand. Sarah

Wendell provides a supporting view and suggests "they [paperback romances] are not always something that you are comfortable holding in your hand in public" and the digital and marketing director of Mills & Boon, Tim Cooper, admits that "part of the appeal of digital reading is that nobody necessarily knows what you're reading" (Masters 2012). The Chief Financial Officer Barb Perfetti also shares a similar view that with eBooks, "it's easier to check out some naughty little title online than in a brick-and-mortar store where your pastor could step up in line behind you" (Bosman 2010). The digitised versions of novels and the reading privacy this offers have contributed to an increase in the sales of eBooks, which have now surpassed paperback novels (Masters 2012). Additionally, digital platforms provide another profitable avenue as the company "takes a percentage of the profits each time a book is downloaded" (Shaw 2014). Moreover, unlike books, eBooks do not have a physical presence. Due to the electronic format of the romance novels, there are no printing costs (Levine 2012: 166).

The marketing strategies apply not only to the paperback books but also to the different promotional channels where these products are advertised, such as the company's websites[10] and different blogs.[11] The use of the internet and the "smart" structure of the company's websites facilitates the promotion, viewings, and sales of novels. Eric Allen and Jerry Fjermestad postulate that e-commerce is beneficial for both consumers and companies. First, consumers can search and collect information on the company's products effortlessly and "at virtually no cost" (2001: 14). Second, by visiting the company's website, consumers can locate the product they are interested in without having to navigate through other sites (17). Third, the internet offers a cost-effective way for the company to create a "link" with the consumer (18). In an attempt to increase the profits, maintain a global status and attract readership across different ages, cultures, and ethnicities, Harlequin and Mills & Boon has come up with an innovative categorisation of its products. On the British website, the romance novels are catalogued by series. There are seven series: Modern, Historical, Medical, Desire, True Love, Heroes, and Dare. There are also Great Value Bundles and Anthologies where novels are brought together on the basis of the themes featured in their pages. Similarly, on the Canadian website,[12] the books are listed on the basis of their series, categories, imprints, and authors. Here, the series are a lot more than the ones that appear on the website of Mills & Boon, for example, Harlequin Historical, Harlequin Medical Romance, Harlequin Heartwarming, Harlequin Presents, and Love Inspired. Correspondingly, some of the categories presented on the Canadian website are Action & Adventure, Asian American, Christian Fiction, Detective, and so forth.

The "smart" structure of the websites allows novels to be featured in more than one group. Thus, the consumer is lured towards browsing more than one category and this maximises the exposure of the book. Webpages from companies, such as Harlequin and Mills & Boon, Amazon, and Netflix, also provide follow-on online services and use "recommender systems" (to further advertising exposure) (Bobadilla et al. 2011: 14609). These systems record consumers' interests, last purchases, views of products, and ratings. By doing so, companies are "emulating each step of [the customers'] behavior insofar as is possible" only to later identify other users with similar interests and then offer the latter's choice as "recommendations of elements that have not [been] rated yet (assuming in this way that they are new to [the customers]) and which have been rated the best by the group of users with similar tastes" (14609). Not only do these recommender systems increase the viewings of the products and their sales but also they attract readers with similar, but not identical, interests. For instance, one novel may cater for one's fantasy and also paranormal reading interests. Such is the case of Rhyannon Byrd's novel entitled *Dark Wolf Returning* (published in August 2014), which is featured in both genres.

There are a few additional, noteworthy points with reference to the company website: it facilitates the promotion of a globalised brand image of the publishers. Since 2000, its website has been "refined and adopted by Harlequin-Mills & Boon offices around the world, producing an internationally consistent brand identity and location online" (McWilliam 2009: 142). The existence of online communities and blogs provided by Harlequin and Mills & Boon assists in ensuring readers' satisfaction. These online spaces offer romance fans the opportunity to discuss, read posts, comment, and give feedback regarding new books. The feedback mechanism contributes to a sense of community in which open communications are encouraged and customer engagement is enhanced (Mangold and Faulds 2009: 361). Additionally, romance readers have the opportunity to receive information about new releases of novels and participate in various events – for example, 2022 Romance Reading Challenge.[13]

Also, social media pages (e.g. Facebook, Twitter, Pinterest, Instagram, and YouTube)[14] have been created by Harlequin and Mills & Boon to maximise readers' interaction with the authors and publishers. According to Glynn Mangold and David Faulds, social media functions as a channel of communication between the companies and customers (2009: 358) and aids a customer-centric approach. Jennifer Enderlin, the associate publisher of St. Martin's paperbacks, also stresses the usefulness of social media in the book industry and states that "now you read a book, you go to the Web site, you chat with the author, you chat with your friends" (Enderlin in Danford et al. 2003). However, it should be noted here that this is not the company's first attempt to construct a community of readers. Prior to its online presence, Mills & Boon's "Rose of Romance Book Club" was another way of bringing the readers together. Every new members of this club received six new titles for free (Philips 1990: 149).

Furthermore, another marketing strategy used to promote the brand and also engage readers was the creation and launch of "The Chatsfield" in May 2014.[15] This was a project that featured a fictional online hotel which hosts a variety of storylines. According to the publisher, "a digital story isn't just an ebook or an ebook with hyperlinks or video added" but rather an interactive "social storytelling" hub where readers could become part of the story by engaging with the characters, adding, and also altering the plot of the progressive narrative (Flood 2014). The different stories created by the readers were available on Twitter, Facebook, YouTube and other blogs. On the basis of the aforementioned discussion of the marketing strategies that Harlequin and Mills & Boon employ, the publishers have "shown a marked willingness to work within, not against, the changing times, in this way applying innovative and forward-thinking solutions to the exigent conditions of the post-millennial book trade" (Tapper 2014: 251).

To conclude, since the two publishing houses joined, the company has gained a global status and both marketing/distributing practices and their use of innovative marketing techniques and technology have consistently evolved in line with market trends and reading habits. Romance fiction is a multibillion industry sustained by 200 in the UK and a further 1,300 worldwide successful authors (Gillmor 2009) and supported by a continuously growing readership that is responsive to sophisticated commercial marketing and distribution techniques. In other words, it is the amalgamation of marketing expertise and know-how, the customer-centric approach, the identification and targeting of niche markets, the diversification of the products, and a good understanding of consumers' demands that have earned Harlequin and Mills & Boon the status of a global publisher.

The ongoing success and growing number of sales are indicative of high consumer demand and a healthy romance genre. It is then no surprise that romance caught the attention of scholars and academics and quickly became the recipient of both negative and positive criticism over the years. However, discussing the romance genre should not be a matter of choosing a side in this argument. For this reason, this book is not an encomium on these narratives; neither a criticism against them. Rather, its primary aim is to offer a re-reading of post-millennial romance novels as a process of making meaning (of these narratives) through a twenty-first-century context. Specifically, its scope is to investigate a selection of popular romance novels and their *involvement* in the construction of the romantic masculinities. To do so, a poststructuralist stance is taken.

The rationale behind the choice of poststructuralism as a theoretical perspective for this analysis is based on its ability to view texts as open-ended; this is an attempt to discover and produce new interpretations and meanings, and also to make sense of the world through diverse perspectives (Baxter 2002: 5). Taking this into account, universal statements about poststructuralism are not made as this would contradict its ability to challenge master narratives. Similarly, generalised statements about romance novels are avoided. In addition, this investigation is not a comparison of post-millennial and pre-millennial romance novels. Rather, it is a *snapshot* of a selection of post-millennial romance novels published between 2000 and 2015. This investigation is an attempt to advance an agenda of how the concept of masculinity is projected within the post-millennial romance novel context. The use of poststructuralism here facilitates an understanding of how notions (in this case masculinity) can carry various, and at times opposing, connotations that may change over time (Weedon [1987] 1997: 24). Under a poststructuralist lens, and to address the scope of the book, this analysis is placed in a twenty-first-century context.

More specifically, it follows a close textual analysis approach and a gender reading of romance narratives; it explores the masculine subject as portrayed in the chosen corpus. Moreover, it attempts to discover the extent to which these novels embrace and reinforce master narratives (i.e. hegemonic masculinity) and put these conventions under stress and hint at their disruption.

For the purposes of this book, rather than selecting novels from the wide variety of romance subgenres, the corpus was chosen from the Contemporary Romance subgenre. What makes this subgenre distinctive for this investigation is that it embodies "novels with contemporary settings [. . .], these novels usually focus on the attempts of characters to find success and fulfilment professionally, personally, and romantically" (Ramsdell 2012: 47). Contemporary romance novels appear to be "in line with current social trends" (47) and make references to issues of contemporary relevance that were once dismissed as taboos (e.g. prostitution and homosexuality). This subgenre, what was formerly considered taboo, has now

> become commonplace and characters who were considered unacceptable or too realistic for the genre (e.g. the hero or heroine deeply wounded by abuse, war, rape, torture, or other devastating tragedy; the ex-convict or alcoholic hero or heroine; the variously disabled hero or heroine; the bad girl heroine; the gay friend or couple) now rarely raise an eyebrow.
>
> (49)

For instance, such a character is Tiffany Davis, the heroine in *The Ultimate Seduction* (Dani Collins 2014); after a car accident, she is left with scars on her face and body. Theo Pantelidis, the hero in *What the Greek Wants Most*, was abducted and tortured as a child by the heroine's father (Maya Blake 2014). Moreover, the decision and selection of novels from this subgenre are a response to a call made by Sarah Frantz and Eric Selinger,[16] prominent scholars in the field, who stress the need to "turn away from accounts of the genre 'as a whole'" (Frantz and Selinger 2012: 14–15). Instead, they propose that researchers focus on issues such as "conventions, *subgenres*, and audiences that scholars have yet to explore" (15) (emphasis added).

The Contemporary Romance subgenre is wide-ranging and consists of different series (e.g. Harlequin Medical Romance, Dare, Desire, Intrigue, Presents/Modern, Romantic Suspense, and Heartwarming) and the task of analysing it in its entirety is beyond the scope of this book. Instead, the decision was made to examine *part* of the subgenre and chose the Harlequin Presents/Mills & Boon Modern series (henceforth Modern). The Modern series was launched in 2000. In light of this, the selected novels were published between 2000 and 2015. The Modern series is "a series of short, sensual 'escapist romantic fantasies' in which characters are swept off to exotic, glamorous locales where they can blissfully give in to love" (Ramsdell 2012: 108). This series was chosen on the basis of the premise that it is the most successful, popular, and prolific sub-category of the contemporary romance series (Elliott 2015: 1) and that its scope is "to develop relevant, contemporary issues, which touch the lives of today's women" (Mettee et al. 2006: 677). A further reason was the dearth of research carried out on the Modern series (Elliott 2015: 6). Other category romance series have tended to receive greater attention to date. For example, there are studies that focus on inspirational romance novels (Barrett 2003; McClain 2002), erotic (Coles and Shamp 1984; Selinger 2015), historical (Hughes 1993; Burge 2016; Kamblé 2014), and paranormal romances (McClain 2000) to name a few.

Additionally, this is also an exciting period for romance scholarship as increased scholarly attention, debate, discussions, and criticism have emerged. This "third wave of scholarship" (Frantz and Selinger 2012: 7) – which was triggered in 2003–2004 by the works of Pamela Regis (*A Natural History of the Romance Novel*) and Juliet Flesch (*From Australia with Love*) – contributed to the expansion of the romance field by bringing scholars together and sparked a series of conferences on the genre of romance. In 2005, the Romance Writers of America introduced an academic research grant to aid further the romance field, Laura Vivanco established a collaborative academic blog (Teach Me Tonight) and Sarah Frantz established the first organisation of romance The International Association for the Study of Popular Romance (10).

Chapter 1 discusses the concepts of "hegemony" and "hegemonic masculinity", and by drawing from various scholars in the field of masculinities and popular fiction, a definition is formed. Moreover, this chapter sets the theoretical background for the analysis of the "Modern" romance novels examined in this book. Chapters 2 and 3 focus on the projections of the romance hero as an embodiment of different dominant forms of masculinity. Specifically, Chapter 2, informed by Connell's ideas on "managerial masculinity", discusses the transnational business masculinity portrayed by the romantic hero and the elements that constitute it, while Chapter 3 investigates the characteristics that hint towards a hybrid masculinity (a notion borrowed from Demetriou). Chapter 4 explores the notions of body and beauty that surround popular romance heroes in relation to mass media and its construction of dominant masculinities. Chapter 5 examines the concept of "lesser masculinities" in popular romance fiction, their raison d'être, and function.

Notes

1. *Arrows from the Dark* by Sophie Cole was the first romance and also the first ever book to be published by Mills & Boon.
2. Bourdieu compares high-cultural production (e.g. opera) to low-cultural production of works of art (e.g. soap opera). He describes the latter as heteronomous due to their lack of originality and their ability to please the mass audience.
3. On its website, Mills & Boon states that its "novels are published in over 150 countries and 6 continents, in over 30 different languages, with a book sold every two seconds, worldwide" (www.millsandboon.com.au/pages/about-us).
4. Harlequin Reader Service still operates to this day (www.readerservice.com/content/).
5. The content may also be adapted to fit the guidelines of series. For instance:

    The Love Inspireds severely restrict representations of female sexual agency and even female sexual desire. [. . .] Moreover, the Love Inspireds also restrict representations of female social agency, privileging not a social order grounded in some sort of sexual equality, as is the case with other Harlequin romances, but instead privileging a social order grounded in reactionary, fundamentalist Christian values.

    (Darbyshire 2002: 76)

6. This is a nonfiction book of two parallel autobiographies: that one of Angela Bassett and Courtney Vance. The book focuses on their coming together as a couple as well as notions of marriage, balance between work and home, and having children through surrogacy. When Harlequin bought the publishing assets of a company called BET Books, the title came into their possession and was first published in 2007 under the Kimani series.
7. Harlequin Desire is still in print, whereas Silhouette's Sensual Romance was replaced by Harlequin Blaze in 2005. In 2007, Silhouette's Sensation series was merged with Silhouette Intrigue to form Mills & Boon Intrigue. Production for both Harlequin Blaze and Mills & Boon Intrigue series ceased in 2017.

Introduction 13

8. According to Sheth et al. "Customer-centric marketing emphasizes understanding and satisfying the needs, wants, and resources of individual consumers and customers rather than those of mass markets or market segments" (2000: 56–57).
9. Harlequin Romance Report (2012). Some of the other key trends to emerge from this report are that from a sample of 1,500 women, 91% believed that dating rules have become more flexible. The report is also contradictory as it claims that 89% of women claim that the best days for love in their lives are still yet to come. Interestingly over half of women (55%) believe that romance was important for their love relationships, and in fact 70% claimed that it supported them having a better state of health and wellbeing. In addition, the traditional charms of a man (e.g. sense of humour – 82% – and a killer smile, 57%) are the most popular turn-ons for women.
10. www.millsandboon.co.uk/ and www.harlequin.com/
11. https://blog.millsandboon.co.uk/, https://blog.harlequin.com/
12. www.harlequin.com/
13. https://blog.harlequin.com/2022/03/join-our-2022-romance-reading-challenge/
14. www.facebook.com/harlequinbooks, https://twitter.com/harlequinbooks, www.pinterest.com/harlequinbooks/, www.instagram.com/harlequinbooks/, www.youtube.com/c/millsandboon
15. "The Chatsfield" hotel project ended on 2 August 2014. For more information, see: www.telegraph.co.uk/technology/news/10804559/Mills-and-Boon-launches-digital-series-The-Chatsfield.html and www.youtube.com/watch?v=VV2K5YpojJA
16. Eric Selinger is the president of the International Association for the Study of Popular Romance as well as the executive editor of the *Journal of Popular Romance Studies*.

Bibliography

Allen, E. & Fjermestad, J. (2001) E-commerce marketing strategies: an internal framework and case analysis. *Logistics Information Management*, 14, 14–23.

Andriani, L. (2009) Harlequin books hits 60. *Publishers Weekly*, 19 March [Online]. Available at: www.publishersweekly.com/pw/by-topic/industry-news/publisher-news/article/9603-harlequin-books-hits-60.html

Barrett, R. (2003) Higher love: what women gain from Christian romance novels. *Journal of Religion and Popular Culture*, 4 (1). Available online: www.utpjournals. press/doi/abs/10.3138/jrpc.4.1.001

Baxter, J. (2002) A juggling act: a feminist post-structuralist analysis of girls' and boys' talk in the secondary school classroom. *Gender and Education*, 14, 5–19.

Blake, M. (2014) *What the Greek wants most*. Richmond, Surrey: Harlequin Mills & Boon.

Bobadilla, J., Hernando, A., Ortega, F. & Bernal, J. (2011) A framework for collaborative filtering recommender systems. *Expert Systems with Application*, 38, 14609–23.

Bodsworth, C. (2004) How Mills and Boon turned to manga comics. *BBC*, 12 April [Online]. Available at: http://news.bbc.co.uk/1/hi/magazine/3614229.stm

Borland, S. (2008) Mills & Boon books translated into Polish. *The Telegraph*, 28 January [Online]. Available at: www.telegraph.co.uk/news/uknews/1576761/Mills-and-Boon-books-translated-into-Polish.html

Bosman, J. (2010) Lusty tales and hot sales: romance e-Books thrive. *The New York Times*, 8 December [Online]. Available at: www.nytimes.com/2010/12/09/books/09romance.html?_r=0

Bourdieu, P. (1991) *Language and symbolic power*. Cambridge: Polity.

———. (1993) *The field of cultural production: essays on art and literature*. Translated by Randal Johnston. Cambridge: Polity Press.

———. (1996) *The rules of art: genesis and structure of the literary field*. Translated by Susan Emanuel. Stanford: Stanford University Press.

Burge, A. (2016) *Representing difference in the medieval and modern orientalist romance*. Hamprshire: Palgrave Macmillan.

Cohn, J. (1988) *Romance and the erotics of property: mass-market fiction for women*. Durham: Duke University Press.

Coles, C. & Shamp, M. (1984) Some sexual, personality, and demographic characteristics of women readers of erotic romances. *Archives of Sexual Behavior*, 13, 187–209.

Collins, D. (2014) *The ultimate seduction*. Richmond, Surrey: Harlequin Mills & Boon.

Creed, B. (2003) *Media matrix: sexing the new reality*. Sydney: Allen & Unwin.

Danford, N., Dyer, L., Holt, K. & Rosen, J. (2003) Toujours l'amour. *Publishers Weekly*, 01 December [Online]. Available at: www.publishersweekly.com/pw/print/20031201/29546-toujours-l-amour.html

Dredge, S. (2014) Bodice-ripping Mills & Boon novels? There's an app for that. *The Guardian*, 26 February [Online]. Available at: www.theguardian.com/technology/2014/feb/26/mills-and-boon-app-iphone-ipad

Dystel, O. (1980) Mass market publishing: more observations, speculations and provocations. *Publishers Weekly*, 218, 18–25.

Elliott, J. (2015) Whole genre sequencing. *Digital Scholarship in the Humanities*. Available Online: https://dsh.oxfordjournals.org/content/early/2015/09/02/llc.fqv034

Flesch, J. (2004) *From Australia with love: a history of modern Australian popular romance novels*. Perth: Curtin University Books.

Flood, A. (2012) Mills & Boon turns heat up Fifty Shades with erotica titles. *The Guardian*, 4 July [Online]. Available at: www.theguardian.com/books/2012/jul/04/mill-boon-erotica-titles

———. (2014) Mills & Boon announces "totally new" digital storytelling format. *The Guardian*, 6 May [Online]. Available at: www.theguardian.com/books/2014/may/06/mills-and-boon-new-digital-storytelling-formant

Frantz, S. & Selinger, E. (2012) (eds.) *New approaches to popular romance fiction: critical essays*. Jefferson, North Carolina and London: McFarland & Company Inc.

Gelder, K. (2004) *Popular fiction: the logics and practices of a literary field*. London and New York: Routledge.

Gillmor, D. (2009) That old flame: after sixty years, Harlequin romance books are still enslaving readers. What's their secret? *The Walrus*, May [Online]. Available at: http://thewalrus.ca/that-old-flame/

Graves, J. (2014) Beyond Valentine's day: the romance novel in the evolving world of publishing. *LIANZA Conference*. Auckland, 12–15 October 2014, 1–7.

Grescoe, P. (1996) *The merchants of Venus: inside Harlequin and the empire of romance*. Vancouver: Raincoast Books.

Hartley, J. (2005) Creative industries. In Hartley, J. (ed.) *Creative industries*. Malden: Blackwell, 1–40.
Hughes, H. (1993) *The historical romance*. London: Routledge.
Ireland, R. D., Hoskinsson, R. & Hitt, M. (2006) *Understanding business strategy: concepts and cases*. United States: Cincinnati, Ohio. Thomson South-Western.
Jensen, M. (1984) *Love's sweet return: the Harlequin story*. Bowling Green: Bowling Green State University Press.
Kamblé, J. (2014) *Making meaning in popular romance fiction: an epistemology*. New York: Palgrave Macmillan.
Kotler, P. (2000) *Marketing management*. Boston: Pearson Custom Publishing.
Levine, R. (2012) *Free ride: how digital parasites are destroying the culture business, and how the culture business can fight back*. London: Vintage.
Mangold, G. & Faulds, D. (2009) Social media: The new hybrid element of the promotion mix. *Blue Horizons*, 52, 357–65.
Markert, J. (1985). Romance publishing and the production of culture. *Poetics*, 14, 69–93.
Masters, T. (2012) Ebooks: is digital opening up a new chapter for publishing? *BBC*, 10 May [Online]. Available at: www.bbc.co.uk/news/entertainment-arts-17961137
McAleer, J. (1999) *Passion's fortune: the story of Mills & Boon*. Oxford: Oxford University Press.
McClain, T. (2000) Paranormal romance: secrets of the female fantastic. *Journal of the Fantastic in the Arts*, 11 (3), 294–306.
———. (2002) When love is divine: the Christian romance novel. *The Chronicle of Higher Education*, 48. Available online: http://chronicle.com/article/When-Love-Is-Divine-the/11131
McCracken, S. (2012) Reading time: popular fiction and the everyday. In Glover D. & McCracken, S. (eds.) *The Cambridge companion to popular fiction*. Cambridge: Cambridge University Press, 103–21.
McWilliam, K. (2009) Romance in foreign accents: Harlequin-Mills & Boon in Australia. *Continuum: Journal of Cultural & Media Studies*, 23 (2), 137–45.
Mettee, S., Doland, M. & Hall, D. (2006) *The American directory of writer's guidelines*. Sanger: Quill Driver Books/Word Dancer Press.
Milliot, J. (2007) Harlequin gets serious about nonfiction. *Publishers Weekly*, 2 November [Online]. Available at: www.publishersweekly.com/pw/by-topic/industry-news/publisher-news/article/9775-harlequin-gets-serious-about-nonfiction.html
Paizis, G. (2006) Category romance in the era of globalization: the story of Harlequin. In Guttman, A., Hockx, M. & Paizis, G. (eds.) *The global literary field*. Newcastle: Cambridge Scholars Press, 126–51.
Philips, D. (1990) Mills and Boon: the marketing of moonshine. In Tomlinson, A. (ed.) *Consumption, identity, & style: marketing, meanings, and the packaging of pleasure*. London and New York: Routledge, 139–52.
Radway, J. ([1984)] 1991) *Reading the romance: women, patriarchy, and popular literature*. Chapel Hill and London: The University of North Carolina Press.
Ramsdell, K. (2012) *Romance fiction: a guide to the genre*. California: Libraries Unlimited.

Regis, P. (2003) *A natural history of the romance novel*. Philadelphia: University of Pennsylvania Press.

Royle, J., Cooper, L. & Stockdale, R. (1999) The use of branding by trade publishers: an investigation into marketing the book as a brand name product. *Publishing Research Quarterly*, 15 (4), 3–13.

Selinger, E. (2015) Erotica: romance novels. *The international encyclopedia of human sexuality*, 325–68.

Shaw, D. (2014) Why publisher Mills & Boon is romancing the mobile app. *BBC*, 28 April [Online]. Available at: www.bbc.co.uk/news/technology-27131182

Sheth, J., Sisodia, R. & Sharma, A. (2000) The antecedents and consequences of customer-centric marketing. *Journal of the Academy of Marketing Science*, 28 (1), 55–66.

Tapper, O. (2014) Romance and innovation in twenty-first century publishing. *Publishing Research Quarterly*, 30, 249–59.

Thomas, G. (2012) Happy readers or sad ones? Romance fiction and the problems of the media effects model. In Frantz, S. & Selinger, E. (eds.) *New approaches to popular romance fiction: critical essays*. Jefferson, North Carolina and London: McFarland & Company, Inc, 206–17.

Weedon, C. ([1987] 1997) *Feminist practice and poststructuralist theory*. New York: Blackwell.

Wind, Y. (1986) The myth of globalization. *Journal of Consumer Marketing*, 3 (2), 23–6.

Woodard, J. (1998) God starts cleaning up the pulp-romance: Harlequin brings out an "Inspiration" series to feed a growing hunger for religion. *Alberta Report*, 25 (4), 36.

1 Hegemonic Masculinity and the Romance Hero

> The romance hero [is] a *construction*, one that reflects contemporary ideas of masculinity more than any woman's ideal man. The [hero] draws from ideas of masculinity already available in our culture, but modifies them to make him a woman's fantasy, rather than that of a man.
>
> (Zidle 1999: 23)

In the field of gender studies, "hegemonic masculinity" is one of the most cited and discussed concepts. Hegemony is

> a social ascendancy achieved in a play of social forces that extends beyond contests of brute power into the organization of private life and cultural processes. Ascendancy [. . .] is embedded in religious doctrine and practice, mass media content, wage structures, the design of housing, welfare/taxation policies and so forth.
>
> (Connell 1987: 184)

Hegemony refers to the way power functions in constructing our understanding of social relations. In addition, it emphasises the manner in which people accept relations of authority and power and also how individuals repeat them (Butler 2000: 14). What derives from this definition is the perception of hegemonic masculinity as a dominant ideology of masculinity (Connell 2001: 38–9). Its general characteristics (in the contemporary West) are typically associated with "whiteness, location in the middle class, heterosexuality, independence, rationality and educated, a competitive spirit, the desire and the ability to achieve, controlled and directed aggression, as well as mental and physical toughness" (Howson 2012: 60). This desired, idealised masculinity is what the majority of men tend to aspire towards and it functions as an ideal that, by definition, cannot be reached. Therefore, achieving it is impossible. Hegemonic masculinity is

DOI: 10.4324/9781003202837-2

powerful, as a result, because it ensures men's compliance with the system. It does so by preserving traditionally accepted practices (e.g. men as breadwinners and family providers) as important hegemonic masculine principles which in effect contribute to maintaining the continuance of this idealised masculinity (61). This dominant masculinity is also constantly evolving as it is a social construct and "a lived experience" (Donaldson 1993: 646) that is subject to social relations which may vary depending on the time period (Messner and Sabo 1990: 12), social class and profession (Tolson 1977: 81), financial status, and even depending on location, levels of modernisation and globalisation.

Jeff Hearn (2004: 53) notes that various studies have used hegemony as a term in discussions and debates on men, for example, "hegemonic masculinity" (Carrigan et al. 1985), "male hegemony" (Cockburn 1991), and "hegemonic heterosexual masculinity" (Frank 1987). However, to date, the meaning of the term "hegemony" has been ambiguous and the question of who represents hegemonic masculinity remains unanswered. For instance, in a study undertaken in 1990, Connell describes the Australian "iron-man" surfing champion as an example of hegemonic masculinity. However, Mike Donaldson (1993) appears to disagree with the hegemonic model proposed by Connell as his hegemonic status refrains the surfer from acting in ways that his peer considers masculine (drinking, showing off etc.). What scholars (e.g. Martin 1998; Wetherell and Edley 1999) agree on is that the concept does not specify who can be considered as a hegemonic male, or what are the defining characteristics of this type of ideal masculinity. As Stephen Whitehead puts it: "Is it John Wayne or Leonardo DiCaprio; Mike Tyson or Pele? Or maybe, at different times, all of them?" (Whitehead 2002: 93) Taking into account the confusion that surrounds the term, Connell and Messerschmidt (2005: 838) propose that hegemonic masculinity should not be seen as a fixed term referring to a specific model of masculinity as this hinders academics and scholars from acknowledging the social development of masculinity and its definitions.

As a result of the term's ambiguity, scholars mainly focus on how certain forms of masculinity can dominate others. Carrigan et al. conceptualise the term as "a question on how particular groups of men inhabit positions of power and wealth and how they legitimate and reproduce the social relations that generate their dominance" (Carrigan et al. 1987: 179). Connell suggests that it is not of great importance to describe the term but argues that dominant masculinity is "the most honoured or desired in a particular context" (Connell 1995: 77). Across different cultures, this dominant form of masculinity receives its form through the creation of the hero in narratives as one of the ways in which this form of masculinity is promoted. This masculinity is "presented through forms that revolve around heroes:

sagas, ballads, westerns, thrillers" (Connell 1983: 185) and, in the twenty-first century, is experienced by a wide, international audience through the use of mass media.

In Western culture, the hegemonic model of masculinity is successful, heterosexual, aggressive, and rational and takes risks (Connell 1995: 79). Prevailing studies of the popular romance hero seem to present variations of hegemonic masculinity (which echo Connell's definition of the term) and suggest that these forms of idealised masculinity of the West have become synonymous with the dominant Harlequin and Mills & Boon alpha male. For example, Heather Schell points out that the term "alpha male" (commonly used for the Harlequin and Mills & Boon hero) is derived from the natural phenomenon of dominant behaviours among dogs and wolves. Her standpoint derives from evolutionary psychologists who believe that male behaviour can be explained if compared to large predatory mammals that exist in dominating and aggressive packs. "'Alpha' was originally used [. . .] to refer to the dominant individuals in rigidly hierarchical animal societies such as [. . .] primates and wolves" (Schell 2007: 113). The application of this term to the male heroes of romance fiction has its roots in "an amalgam of [. . .] popular ideas about the behaviour of wolves (wolves fight to maintain their place in the pack hierarchy), popular ideas about alpha males (they demand fidelity from their mates), and fantasies about ideal human masculinity (tremendous strength and sex appeal)" (115–6). Schell describes the alpha male as powerful, dominant, wealthy, aggressive, influential, intimidating, and physically strong. Mary Talbot adds sexual allure to the definitions of alpha heroes: they are "embodiments of hegemonic masculinity, presented as desirable, highly eroticised and utterly irresistible" (Talbot 1997: 107).

Laura Vivanco offers an alternative definition for the popular romance hero. In her book *For Love and Money: The Literary Art of Harlequin Mills & Boon Romance* (2011), Laura applies Northrop Frye's five fictional modes to popular romance novels. Since the story of all fictional modes revolves around an individual, it is the power of the hero's actions and the portrayal of the surrounding environment that categorise the novel under one of those mode types. Frye states:

> In literary fictions the plot consists of somebody doing something. The somebody, if an individual, is the hero, and the something he does or fails to do is what he can do, or could have done, on the level of the postulates made about him by the author and the consequent expectations of the audience. Fictions, therefore, may be classified, not morally, but by the hero's power of action, which may be greater than ours, less, or roughly the same.
>
> (Frye 1957: 33)

These modes are the following: (i) mythic, (ii) romantic, (iii) high-mimetic, (iv) low-mimetic, and (v) ironic. The first mode refers to the fictional protagonists who are superior "in *kind* both to other men and to the environment of other men" (33). This hero would be divine and the story about him would have the form of a myth. Although stories of such nature play an important role in literature, they are "outside of the normal literary categories" (33). For Vivanco, popular romance novels could not fall under the mythic mode because they are not "a myth in the common sense of a story about a god" (33).

Based on Frye's fictional modes, in a romantic narrative, the hero should be "superior in *degree* to other men and to his environment" but presented as a human being (33). Nevertheless, "the laws of nature are quite suspended" (33) and although his actions may seem natural to him, they are quite unnatural to the readership. Supernatural and paranormal elements, such as bewitched places or animals, or ghosts, may also be part of the story. According to Vivanco (2011: 32), the Mills & Boon Nocturne[1] line of romances falls into this category as the protagonists of this series are usually vampires, time-travellers, or werewolves with supernatural powers and abilities. She suggests that sometimes both the hero and heroine of the novel may not be human beings but at least one of them is identified as such. High-mimetic literature is when its protagonist is "superior in *degree* to other men but not to his natural environment, the hero is a leader. He has authority, passions, and powers of expression far greater than ours, but what he does is subject both to social criticism and to the order of nature" (Frye 1957: 34). The low-mimetic literary mode alludes to the hero who is "neither superior to other men nor to his natural environment" (34). He is an everyday man and one that most readers would be able to relate to the man-next-door. He is a hero who exists in a common environment and has experiences familiar to the readers, rather than unrealistic or fictitious ones. The ironic mode describes stories in which the hero is

> inferior in power or intelligence to ourselves, so that we have the sense of looking down on a scene of bondage, frustration, or absurdity [. . .]. This is still true when the reader feels that he is or might be in the same situation, as the situation is being judged by the norms of a greater freedom.
>
> (34)

What can be derived from the aforementioned text is that the twenty-first-century heroes depicted in popular romance novels are high-mimetic and bear great resemblance to Connell's hegemonic male ideal; they are pictured as men who have it all. They are handsome, powerful, and successful;

they can exercise authority; they are superior to other men (lesser masculinities that exist in the romance narratives); and they are the ones "that the female of any species will be most intensely attracted to" (McAleer 1999: 149–50).

Hegemonic masculinity is not static but subject to change. Frank Pittman notes that "masculinity is different for each generation" (Pittman 1993: xiv–v). Whereas in the past, the term "man" "conjure[d] up the attendant characteristics of a strong, confident, competitive, and decisive patriarch" (Tragos 2009: 543), this is no longer the case. The man of the twenty-first century is "overly concerned with appearance, fashion, and trends. He is a metrosexual's [*sic*] man" (2009: 545). Or, as Buerkle puts it, he exhibits a "masculinity concerned with aesthetics and other heretofore interests classed as feminine" (Buerkle 2009: 78). The concept of metrosexuality was first introduced by Mark Simpson in 2002 to describe the footballer David Beckham "as a metrosexual *par excellence*, emphasizing the narcissism of culture industry obsession mixed with the heteromasculine assets of desire from straight women and admiration from straight men" (cited in Buerkle 2009: 78). This (metrosexual) man is not afraid to pay great attention to his appearance and to express an interest in fashion and get involved with activities that were once considered as traditionally feminine (Segal 1993: 633–4). Barthel makes the observation that "the growing fascination with appearances, encouraged by advertising, has led to a 'feminization' of culture" (2003: 178). However, this type of masculinity did not conform to the (traditional) ideal masculinity of the past; a man who would show signs of metrosexuality was thought "to be effeminate and not a 'real man'" (171). This perception still exists:

> A well-dressed, well-groomed and "stylish" man still tends to arouse anxieties concerning sexuality and masculinity or the terrifying twosome of the homosexual and the effeminate. Stereotypically, "real" men don't care what they look like and just "throw things on" whilst women go shopping and agonize over matters of self-presentation.
> (Edwards 2003: 142)

A counter-response to this feminised man is the appearance of hypermasculinity. It is an attempt "to reclaim traditional notions of manhood" (Tragos 2009: 546) and a retrograde step towards "an age of rampant chauvinism, where men swagger about in a testosterone rage and women are reduced to sexual ornaments" (Mayer 2003: 512). Hypermasculinity is, as described by Ricciardelli and Clow, the exaggerated presentation of "traditionally" masculine realities (Ricciardelli and Clow 2003: 119) and elements of it can be found in the romance novels examined here (e.g. heterosexuality and sexual allure). The faithfulness of romance authors to the construction of heroes as dominant, aggressive, and at times intimidating for the heroines in the past could be seen as an attempt to avoid any association (of the heroes') with effeminate, queer, or homosexual elements.

The preceding references to other studies indicate that, in the romance context, the hero often receives the form of a hegemonic man. However, as noted earlier, hegemonic masculinity is not a fixed concept. Rather, it is subject to continuous change which allows for the emergence of various dominant masculinities. With this in mind, the analysis of the romance novels examined in this book suggests that to a certain extent the romance hero could be described as a *platform* onto which different forms of dominant masculinity are displayed; a transnational business masculinity (Connell 2005: xxiii) and later, as the plots unfold, a hybrid masculinity (Demetriou 2001). These two forms of masculinity do not replace or negate each other. Rather, when they co-exist, they do so without losing their hegemonic status. The section that follows discusses the transnational business masculinity embodied by the heroes of the chosen corpus. Prior to this, a short definition of the term is necessary. With the world economy, dominant institutions and the globalisation of the neoliberal market in mind, Connell seems to revise the notion of hegemonic masculinity and suggests that transnational business masculinity is closely associated with, and receives an important role, in this context. Furthermore, he asserts that transnational business masculinity can be seen as "a hegemonic masculinity on a world-scale – that is to say, a dominant form of masculinity that embodies, organizes, and legitimates men's domination in the world gender order as a whole" (Connell 2000: 46).

It must be noted that the next chapter focuses on transnational business masculinities in the same way that Connell does. That is, it examines hegemonic masculinity as transnational business masculinity mostly in economic terms (i.e. the hero's financial status, capital, and authority, and the power that comes with it).

Note

1. The Nocturne line is characterised by action-based plots with a high level of sensuality/sexuality. These novels feature powerful and mysterious heroes who face life and death situations. The Nocturne male characters vary from werewolves to shape shifters and from vampires to time-travellers and follow the rules of a paranormal world created by the authors. However, the main focus of these stories is the amorous relationship of the protagonists (and its development) rather than the paranormal element. Romance novels from the Nocturne line are no longer in print (the line was closed in 2017).

Bibliography

Barthel, D. (2003) A gentleman and a consumer. In Maasik, S. & Solomon, J. (eds.) *Signs of life in the USA: reading on popular culture for writers*. New York: Bedford/St. Martin's, 171–81.

Buerkle, W. (2009) Metrosexuality can stuff it: beef consumption as (heteromasculine) fortification. *Text and Performance Quarterly*, 29 (1), 77–93.

Butler, J. (2000) Restaging the universal: hegemony and the limits of formalism. In Butler, J., Laclau, E. & Žižek, S. (eds.) *Contingency, hegemony, universality: contemporary dialogues on the left*. London: Verso, 11–43.

Carrigan, T., Connell, R. & Lee, J. (1985) Towards a new sociology of masculinity. *Theory and Society*, 14 (5): 551–604.

———. (1987) Hard and heavy: toward a new sociology of masculinity. In Kaufman, M. (ed.) *Beyond patriarchy: essays by men on pleasure, power, and change*. Toronto: Oxford University Press.

Cockburn, C. (1991) *In the way of women*. London: Macmillan.

Connell, R. (1983) *Which way is up? Essays on class, sex and culture*. Sydney: Allen and Unwin.

———. (1987) *Gender and power: society, the person and sexual politics*. Sydney: Allen and Unwin.

———. (2000) *The men and the boys*. Cambridge: Polity Press.

———. (2001) The social organization of masculinity. In Whitehead, S. & Barrett, F. (eds.) *The masculinities reader*. Malden: Polity, 30–50.

———. ([1995] 2005) *Masculinities*. Cambridge: Polity Press.

——— & Messerschmidt, J. (2005) Hegemonic masculinity: rethinking the concept. *Gender and Society*, 19 (6), 829–59.

Demetriou, D. (2001) Connell's concept of hegemonic masculinity: a critique. *Theory and Society*, 30, 337–61.

Donaldson, M. (1993) What is hegemonic masculinity? *Theory and Society*, 22, 643–57.

Edwards, T. (2003) Sex, booze and fags: masculinity, style and men's magazines. *The Sociological Review*, 51 (1), 132–46.

Frank, B. (1987) Hegemonic heterosexual masculinity. *Studies in Political Economy*, 24, 159–70.

Frye, N. (1957) *Anatomy of criticism: four essays*. Princeton: Princeton University Press.

Hearn, J. (2004) From hegemonic masculinity to the hegemony of men. *Feminist Theory*, 5 (1), 49–72.

Howson, R. (2012) *Challenging hegemonic masculinity*. London and New York: Routledge.

Martin, P. (1998) Why can't a man be more like a woman? Reflections on Connell's masculinities. *Gender & Society*, 12 (4), 472–74.

Mayer, A. (2003) The new sexual stone age. In Maasik, S. & Solomon, J. (eds.) *Signs of life in the U.S.A.: reading on popular culture for writers*. New York: Bedford/St. Martin's, 512–14.

McAleer, J. (1999) *Passion's fortune: the story of Mills & Boon.* Oxford: Oxford University Press.

Messner, M. & Sabo, D. (1990) *Sport, men, and the gender order.* Campaign, III: Human Kinetics Books.

Ricciardelli, R. & Clow. K. (2013) The portrayal of elements historically associated with masculine and feminine domains in lad and metrosexual men's lifestyle magazines. *Masculinties and Social Change*, 2 (2), 116–45.

Schell, H. (2007) The big bad wolf: masculinity and genetics in popular culture. *Literature and Medicine*, 26 (1), 109–25.

Segal, L. (1 993) Changing men: masculinities in context. *Theory and Society*, 22 (5), 625–41.

Talbot, M. (1997) An explosion deep inside her: women's desire and popular romance fiction. In Harvey, K. & Shalom, C. (eds.) *Language and desire.* London and New York: Routledge, 106–22.

Tolson, A. (1977) *The limits of masculinity.* London: Tavistock.

Tragos, P. (2009) Monster masculinity: honey, I'll be in the garage reasserting my manhood. *The Journal of Popular Culture*, 42 (3), 541–53.

Vivanco, L. (2011) *For love and money: the literary art of the mills & boon romance.* Penrith: HEB.

Wetherell, M. & Edley, N. (1999) Negotiating hegemonic masculinity: imaginary positions and psycho-discursive practices. *Feminism and Psychology*, 9 (3), 335–56.

Zidle, A. (1999) From bodice-ripper to baby-sitter: the new hero in mass-market romance. In Kaler, A. & Johnson-Kurek, R. (eds.) *Romantic conventions.* Bowling Green: Bowling Green University Popular Press.

2 Transnational Business Masculinities in Popular Romance Fiction

In the "Modern" romance novels references to wealth are abundant; wealth is evident in the choice and description of the plot settings – which are expected to be "glitzy, glamorous, international settings to upstage even the swankiest of red-carpet premieres!" – and in the construction of the hero's identity: "there's nothing in the world his powerful authority and money can't buy".[1] Under such guidelines, the "Modern" romances often recount a love story against a backdrop of wealth, assets, luxurious means of transportation, and properties in different exotic locations around the world, aspects that describe the heroes as men of substantial means. For instance, in *Carrying the Greek's Heir* (Sharon Kendrick 2015), Alek Sarantos's

> apartment was everything Ellie had expected and more, although nothing could have prepared her for its sheer size and opulence. Even the relative luxury of the Hog [the luxury hotel where the heroine works as a waitress] paled into insignificance when compared to each high-ceilinged room which seemed to flow effortlessly into the next. Squashy velvet sofas stood on faded silken rugs and everywhere you looked were beautiful objects. On a small table was a box inlaid with mother-of-pearl and a small gilded egg studded with stones of emerald and blue.
>
> (82)

Similarly, Ludovic Petrakis wears a "platinum Rolex that encircle[s] his tanned wrist" (*In Petrakis's Power* 2013: 47), owns an island, and his "private plane [...] was the epitome of the luxury he'd long come to expect when he travelled (79). Xenon's transportation, a chauffeured limousine, and his "homes all over the world" (*The Greek's Marriage Bargain* 2013: 17) are only some of the assets that display his wealth. The heroes featured in these romantic narratives "[possess] a capitalist identity" (Kamblé 2014: 32) and exhibit what Connell describes as "transnational business

DOI: 10.4324/9781003202837-3

masculinity" (2005: 263). This form of dominant masculinity denotes a calculative, ruthless, egocentric masculinity usually exhibited by capitalist entrepreneurs (Connell 2005: 263). These businessmen hold high positions on the corporate ladder and are (or have the potential to be) wealthy (Connell and Wood 2005: 358). These are men who have corporate, economic and social wealth, and power, or in David and Brannon's words, they are "Big Wheel[s]" as their "masculinity is measured by power, success, wealth, and status" (cited in Kimmel 1994: 125–6).

For example, the hero in *In Petrakis's Power* (Cox 2013) is described as follows: "He was as rich as a modern-day Croesus and counted some of the most influential business people in Europe as his friends" (*In Petrakis's Power* 2013: 30). Similarly, Nik Cozakis, the hero featured in *The Cozakis Bride* (Graham 2000), is international, wealthy, and with status and connections in the corporate world. He is the owner of a business empire with an interest in British trade and "wealthy beyond avarice" (8). Drakon Xanthis in *The Fallen Greek Bride* (Porter 2013) is no different to the two former heroes. In this novel, the hero is a "shipping tycoon [. . .] a man obsessed with control and power. A man obsessed with wealth and growing his empire" (9). He is also handsome, aggressive, "a fierce negotiator, a brilliant strategist, an analytical executive, as well as a demanding boss" (59) and possesses the reputation of a successful businessman. Xenon Kanellis in *The Greek's Marriage Bargain* (Kendrick 2013) is a billionaire and also very successful in the corporate world. Such is his success story that "business schools used [it] as a template aimed at people for whom no glass ceiling was too high" (38). Scion of a wealthy family, "he had assumed control of the Kanellis empire after the sudden death of his father – only to discover that the family finances were falling" (38). Through hard work and determination, "he had revitalised the family shipping line and then added a chain of luxury shops" and a "newspaper and publishing house had increased the growing value of his portfolio" (38). This quotation presents the hero's success and wealth "as the benefits of [his] devotion to corporate capitalism" (Kamblé 2014: 35). Kamblé's view would also seem to suggest that there is intent in the romance novels to portray the hero as a corporate capitalist and one who may, to an extent, depict striving to accumulate unprecedented wealth; a similar point alluded to by Connell and Wood who state: "they (businessmen) are, nevertheless, very affluent, and if the younger men prosper in their corporate careers, they can expect to end up wealthy" (2005: 358). Overall, the novels examined here portray heroes whose "wealth, tangible assets and economic power, are basic attributes of [their] masculinity" (Cohn 1988: 127).

The heroes' financial status leads to feelings of power and authority (also traits of the managerial masculinity).[2] As Connell and Wood suggest, power plays a significant role in their everyday life; in order to be successful and survive in this competitive environment (corporate world), they are expected to have the ability to exercise power (2005: 359). In the first few chapters of the novels, the "Modern" Harlequin and Mills & Boon heroes examined here appear to be ruthless and egocentric businessmen with the sole aim to make "what managers value most, profit" (361). Nevertheless, their managerial masculinity is not restricted to the corporate world; as it will be shown further, in some occasions, they see their association with the heroine as another business transaction from which they attempt to profit.

Because of the business-oriented behaviour that they exhibit, these men could be described as "rogue heroes"; rogue heroes are not to be confused with anti-heroes. The term "anti-hero" in M.H. Abrams and Geoffrey Harpham's *Glossary of Literary Terms* is defined as

> the chief person in a modern novel or play whose character is widely discrepant from that of a traditional protagonist, or hero, of a serious literary work. Instead of manifesting largeness, dignity, power, or heroism, the antihero is petty, ignominious, passive, clownish, or dishonest.
> (2014: 16)

Most of the dictionaries and glossaries describe the anti-hero as a wicked and malicious person with qualities that are antithetical to the hero. However, in this book, the term "rogue hero" refers to someone who possesses both heroic and anti-heroic attributes, a protagonist who at times uses paradoxical methods to gain something for his benefit and also helps the heroine. He is what others refer to as Byronic hero (Stein 2009: 74; Reagin 2010: 14). For Sandra Gilbert and Susan Gubar, the Byronic hero "is in most ways the incarnation of worldly male sexuality, fierce, powerful, experienced, simultaneously brutal and seductive, devilish enough to overwhelm the body and yet enough a fallen angel to charm the soul" (2000: 206). Therefore, these contradictory rogue heroes are (initially) portrayed as part-villainous and selfish as they seek to make profit (financial or in the form of pleasure) at the expense (i.e. taking advantage) of the heroines, but they are also part-heroic as they act with the heroines' best interests at heart.

For instance, when Natalie Carr feels resentful about the small amount Ludovic Petrakis is offering for her family hotel, he makes a proposal she cannot refuse. His financial power is used as a representation of his dominance: "I promise you that if you can convincingly act the part of my fiancée while we are in Greece, when we return to the UK I will make sure you are richly rewarded" (*In Petrakis's Power* 2013: 67). He takes advantage of the heroine's financial need and "buys her". This takes the form of an exchange of services, of a business transaction: he will give her more money; she will pretend to be his fiancée. What is titillating here is that the plot suggests that he will have power over her, involving feelings of power eroticisation, domination, and submission: "He suddenly became even more determined to have Natalie masquerade as his fiancée [. . .] Especially as – in the hope of convincing his parents – he fully intended to play the part of devoted fiancé to the hilt" (67). This quotation portrays him as a self-serving dominant hero as he benefits financially from the purchase of the hotel and is also planning to address his sexual urges by seducing her to sleep with him. The heroine, on the other hand, by being paid to play the role of his fiancée, is submitting herself (first financially and then sexually and emotionally) to him.

Nik Cozakis in *The Cozakis's Bride* is also presented as a go-getting, ruthless businessman. However, what is noteworthy here is the submission of Olympia to Nik – a conscious act on her part – when *she* proposes a marriage of convenience to him. She needs his money to offer her mother a better life. It starts with the heroine's own financial submission:

> If you marry me, I'll sign everything over to you [. . .] Not a proper or normal marriage [. . .] just whatever would satisfy my grandfather. I'd stay here in England [. . .] all I'd need is an allowance to live on, and in return you'd have the Manoulis empire all to yourself and not even the annoyance or embarrassment of me being around [. . .]. Think business contract, not marriage.
>
> (2000: 21)

And the negotiation ends with the hero's economic and sexual dominance over the heroine: "You sign a pre-nuptial contract – [. . .] you sign over everything to me on our wedding day" (34–5). "You will have to live in one of my homes [. . .] for a while, at least. You give me a son and heir" (36). Olympia agrees to Nik's terms and seems to "sell" herself and her dowry to him. The reason for this is her mother's living conditions and her deteriorating health. Her mother went against her grandfather's wishes and ran away with her English boyfriend, which resulted in her exclusion from the family and any inheritance. Stripped of any financial support, she now lives in poverty. The hero, in turn, accepts the heroine's offer and by doing so is pictured as a man interested in satisfying his greed for more financial power as well as sexual hunger with the surrender of the heroine. Therefore, he instantly becomes the dominant party of this relationship. His superiority and power over her lasts only for a short period of time; however, as he finally realises his feelings towards the heroine, he decides to leave the past behind and acknowledge her as his wife, his equal and a valuable member of his family.

When Morgan Copeland, the estranged wife of Drakon Xanthis, in *The Fallen Greek Bride* returns home, it is not because of her feelings for the hero. Rather, she has come back to ask for money to pay a ransom and save her father from pirates. As she is left penniless and in a state of despair, the hero grabs the opportunity to gratify his wishes. First, he wants to have his wife back home and regain authority and power over her. Driven by desperation, the heroine says, "I knew you'd mock me, humiliate me. I knew when I flew here, you'd make it difficult, but I came anyway, determined whatever I had to do to help my father. You'll let me plead with you, you'll let me beg" (Porter 2013: 14) and "Is that what you're asking me to do? Am I to go onto my knees in front of you, and plead my case? Is that what it would take to win your assistance?" (17) Second, he wants to "dominate" her emotionally and sexually. His plan (to make her desire him) seems to be successful as later on Morgan catches herself thinking of him: "What sane woman wanted to be ravished? What kind of woman ached to be tied up and taken? Tasted?" (95) and "If only she could go to him, and beg for him to help her, beg him to give her release. Beg for pleasure. She'd happily crawl for him, crawl to him" (96). In a sense, by admitting her sexual attraction to him, she makes herself vulnerable and submits herself to the hero and he receives the long yearned sexual and emotional domination over her. Her submission to him has the form of a business transaction, which he seals in a despotic way: "Undress. [. . .] I want to see my wife. It doesn't seem like much to ask for, not after giving you seven million dollars" (100). He is lending her the money, she must obey, and therefore his wishes are granted. At the end of the novel, the hero undergoes an evolution. The transformation of his despotic and authoritative nature to love and affection combined with his emotional development seem to be in conformity with the heroine's emotional needs. This plotline echoes the apparent old-fashioned relationship where the woman is under the authority of the man; an authority which later becomes love. This transformation of the hero hints at a revised version of hegemonic masculinity (i.e. hybridity, which is addressed further in the chapter) and highlights the conventionality that characterises the novels.

Xenon Kanellis in *The Greek's Marriage Bargain* is also a self-serving hero who is using his money, male power, and reputation to get his wife, Lex, back into his life. Lex's brother, Jason, is addicted to gambling, an addiction that has resulted in trouble several times in the past. On this occasion, he has borrowed a large amount of money that he needs to return against Xenon and Lex's name. Lex operates a small jewellery firm and does not have the financial means to help him. The hero comes to the rescue with a proposition: he will pay off the debt if she temporarily returns to him as his wife.

In the four novels discussed so far, hegemonic (business) masculinity is highlighted through the demonstration of power, wealth, and authority, which place the heroes in a position of superiority over the heroines. As the heroines are helpless and distressed, they have no option but to submit to their masculinity and accept a lower position in the hierarchy of gender power and relations. Xenon's intentions behind this offer are far from genuine: he is not helping her out of the goodness of his heart. Rather, he needs to restore his reputation as a successful man in all aspects of life:

> My marriage is the only thing in my life which could be considered a failure. [. . .] I don't like failure – perceived or otherwise- and it will make my grandmother happy to see us together again. She believes in marriage. At the end of her life it will please her to discover that her favourite grandson is back with his wife.
>
> (Kendrick 2013: 27)

When she refuses his offer, the hero shows his ruthlessness by turning his business arrangement into some sort of a threat: "Then I throw your brother to the wolves" (28). The heroes' wealth both liberates and imprisons the heroines. It sets them free from any financial burdens but simultaneously condemns them by strengthening their dependence on men. Also, the much-needed financial aid that the heroines receive from the heroes gives the latter the opportunity to exercise control and authority over the former and reinforces their (heroes') dominant masculinity. With this argument, the hero uses his masculinity to achieve his self-gratification. Feeling entrapped, and with no other alternatives, the heroine is obliged to do as she is told. It is the hero's representation as a villain that titillates the readers. Familiar with the romance structure (the hero's feminisation which occurs later and the reassurance for an optimistic ending), the readers enjoy the temporary submission of the heroine.

The heroes featured earlier are depicted as calculating, rogue businessmen who strive to gain pleasure, satisfy their (financial, sexual) wishes, and gain profit in various forms. Furthermore, their (corporate) success, and subsequently the wealth and power that come with it, places them in an advantageous position which gives them the opportunity to exercise power and dominate the heroine. Their business mindset becomes apparent from their encounter with the heroine as they see these meetings as an exchange of services; these capitalist heroes apply the "same set of skills to acquire a wife as [they do] money" (Kamblé 2014: 59). They "conform to a vision of masculinity that is hegemonic, heterosexual, deeply committed to capitalist and bourgeois success" (Allan 2016: 37) and may use any means necessary to get what they want. However, over the course of the novel, they seem to abort the tyrannical aspects of their personality, become thoughtful and caring, and finally acknowledge their feelings for the heroines. It is at this stage when the heroes' "rogueness" abates and their (well-concealed) gallant intentions are made apparent. Most frequently, romance fiction narratives are stories that focus on the uneven power dynamics between the protagonists. As in most novels, it is the hero who "is the most important challenge the heroine must face and conquer" (Krentz 1992: 108). All four romance stories seem to start with the heroine's emotional and sexual (forced or voluntary) submission/surrender but soon power and authority change hands. Once the hero and heroine overcome the "barrier",[3] that is, the reasons that keep them apart (e.g. a misunderstanding), the hero admits his love to the heroine. With the declaration of his love, the transformation of the hero occurs: his managerial masculinity remains intact; he is still wealthy, successful, and powerful in the corporate arena, but, on a more personal level, he relinquishes his dominant self, position, and authoritative power; and becomes sensitive, loving, caring, and understanding.

Once his modification is complete, he invites the heroine into his own world. With this invitation comes the empowerment of the heroines. Feeling empowered by the hero's submission and his declaration of love are not the only benefits for the romance heroine. She desires not just the hero but she also wants "authority itself, the power and autonomy the social system denies women" (Cohn 1988: 5). As she brings the hero to his knees – through a betrothal to him – access to his wealth, power, and enhanced status is gained (Lee 2008: 61–2). Nevertheless, this should not come as a surprise as the idea of gaining status via marriage is quite a relatively well-established representation of marriage and love. The reconstruction of the hero's personality from a dominant and authoritative individual to one described as caring, understanding, and sensitive signals the emergence of a hybrid masculine bloc.

Prior to discussing this form of masculinity, elements that reinforce his business masculinity will be explored in the next section.

Press and Fame

In the novels examined here, fame appears to be a common element shared by twenty-first-century "Modern" heroes. Their acquired fame, most of the time negative and toxic, is derived from their representation in the press. Prior to discussing fame and its impact on the romance hero, the terms "celebrity" and "celebrification" (the process of becoming a celebrity) (Jerslev and Mortensen 2016; Turner 2010; Rojek 2001) will be discussed. In the twenty-first-century context of celebrity culture, the term "celebrity" is no longer used to define someone known and recognised for his or her epic achievements (Drake and

Miah 2010: 50–1). Rather, it refers to the representation of this person in the mass media and publicity. In other words, an individual is conceived as a celebrity due to their public image and appearances rather than their skills or performances in a specific arena. Chris Rojek (2001: 17) suggests that there are three diverse types of "celebrification": "ascribed" celebrity, which refers to individuals who acquire fame through lineage (e.g. the actor and rapper Jaden Smith, son of the more famous actor Will Smith); "achieved" celebrity, which is the result of one's own accomplishments and endeavours; and "attributed" celebrity, which derives from the focus and concentration of the media on an individual (i.e. participants in television shows – for example Kim Kardashian). The latter form of celebrification refers to individuals who are famous only based on their "well-knownness" (Boorstin 1961: 57; Rojek 2001: 18). Regardless of the type of celebrification of an individual, a paradox still remains in that celebrities live and operate in both "domains", namely the private, amongst other common people, and the exclusive (public) domain of publicity and notability (Drake and Miah 2010: 54). Therefore, in the media, they are usually represented in two ways: as simple and common individuals, a strategy that reveals them as approachable and helps people identify with them, and also as celebrities and idols (an image unachievable for common individuals) (Dyer 1979).

In the context of romance novels analysed here, the celebrification of the heroes is generally linked with the transnational business masculinity that they exhibit. The heroes' conception as "achieved" celebrities derives from the power, wealth, and status they have acquired through their activities in the corporate arena. Leonidas Vassalio in *A Greek Escape* is such an example. Despite being described in a negative light, it is through his managerial masculinity that he attracts the attention of the press and receives a celebrity status:

> A couple of the high-ranking executives he had trusted to run one of his UK subsidiaries, along with a unscrupulous lawyer, had reneged on a verbal promise over a development deal and given the Vassalio Group bad press. [. . .] That ordinary people had been lied to and were having their homes bulldozed from under them didn't sit comfortably on his conscience. Nor did being accused of riding roughshod over people without giving a thought to their needs, breaking up communities so as to profit from multi-million-pound sports arenas and retail/leisure complexes and expand on Vassalio's ever-increasing assets.
>
> (16–17)

The images of "ruthless", "unscrupulous", and "a profiteer" created by the media portray him as a businessman fuelled by profiteering activities and oblivious to the people that are left homeless. This depiction of transnational business masculinity appears to corroborate Kamblé's view who states that "qualities such as cleverness and ruthlessness [are] characteristics borrowed heavily from the popular characterisation of CEOs and CFOs" (2014: 32). Moreover, this passage typifies Connell and Wood's description of the managerial men who state that "power [. . .] is a large reality in their [the transnational businessmen's] lives" as they "deploy huge assets and affect large numbers of people" (2005: 359).

Jake from *A Girl Less Ordinary* (Ashton 2012) is another hero who is pictured as an "achieved" celebrity; a status he has acquired due to his business (he owns a smart phone company) and his successful corporate activities. Unlike Leonidas Vassalio, who is represented as ruthless, Jake Donner is praised by the press: "his name splashed across everything from articles of terribly serious business analysis to the trashiest of gossip magazines. And he was always linked to impressive phrases: *Internet Visionary* for one. Or *Web Evangelist*. Even *The Bill Gates of His Generation*" (2012: 26). Similarly to the hero discussed earlier, Jake's wealth and status – which constitute elements of his managerial masculinity – reinforce his celebrity identity. The tabloid magazines refer to him as an "infamous multimillionaire recluse. Number two in *Headline* magazine's list in Australia's most intriguing people. Number *one* in *Lipstick*'s most eligible bachelors" (19).

In addition, the heroes are also "attributed" celebrities whose "well-knownness" is gained mostly from references to their personal life (in this case, encounters with women). An example that links mass media and the construction (or in this case destruction) of Leonidas's public image is the focus on his relationship with American model/actress Esmeralda Leigh who publicly claims that Leonidas is the father of her child: "It was she who had called him unscrupulous, when he had challenged the proof of his paternity" (*A Greek Escape* 2013: 122). Esmeralda's claims, although untrue, give room to the press to generate a negative representation of the hero as a heartless man unwilling to shoulder responsibility and admit to the paternity of a child. In this context, a negative public image appears to affect and destroy "both visual pictures/representations and reputational status" (Penfold 2004: 291). Nevertheless, what reinforces the heroine's doubts about the hero is the repetition of his already-established and unalterable negative image by the press. In the twenty-first century, where "seeing is believing" (Urry 2000: 180), the hero's image is repeatedly calumniated by the mass media. As a result of a continuous defamatory portrayal of the hero by the press, the heroine is influenced, adapts to this view (of him), and is now convinced "Esmeralda was right. You *are* unscrupulous!" (*A Greek Escape* 2013: 122).

Similarly, Jake's status as an "attributed" celebrity is also emphasised through Georgina's (his one and only short term relationship) press statements "Jake Donner – what you see is all you get" (*A Girl Less Ordinary* 2012: 182). Therefore, the press picture him as a man incapable of having any feelings. He also acknowledges his emotional inaccessibility: "I don't feel like that you know? I don't have those feelings. I don't get love" (182). However, regardless of the negative press, these heroes may attract and the damage their image may suffer, they remain perceived as famous and celebrities due to their wealth and status. Despite Jake's characterisation (by both his ex and press) as an empty, emotionally distant man, the hero is first and foremost described on the basis of his managerial success:

> *Spotted! Jake Donner, multimillionaire founder of Armada Software, canoodling with a mystery woman during the launch of Armada's first smart phone on Friday! No word yet on the identity of the lucky lady, but whoever convinced this famously private bachelor to participate in such a public display of affection needs to tell this gossip columnist her secrets. And by the way, faithful readers, have you seen Jake's new look? One word for you: Phwoar!*
>
> (194)

His accomplishments, name of company, and nature of business occupy half a sentence; however, this information is used as a point of reference and marker of his managerial masculinity and his "achieved" celebrity status.

In the same vein, the hero in *A Greek Escape* is still perceived as "Leonidas, Chief Executive of the Vassalio Group. International tycoon. The grandest player in the company man's arena" (2013: 135). The heroine's opinion about the hero does not differ much from the way he is represented by the press: in her eyes, he is "Leonidas Vassalio, hardened billionaire, powerful magnate" (161). When the heroine confides to a friend that she has a relationship with the hero, she receives the following reaction: "Honestly, Kayla! Do you *know* how rich he is?" (154).

Similarly to Jake and Leonidas, Alek Sarantos (*Carrying the Greek's Heir*) is also an "achieved" celebrity. To the press he is known as "one of the world's richest men who usually hangs out with supermodels and heiresses" (Kendrick 2015: 29) and a ruthless businessman "of steel, with a heart to match" (29–30). His fame relies heavily on his corporate activities and achievements. However, even as the press focuses on his private life and the hero receives an "attributed" celebrification, there is still an emphasis on elements of his managerial masculinity:

> One of London's most eligible bachelors may be off the market before too long. The Midas touch billionaire, known for his love of

supermodels and heiresses, was spotted in a passionate embrace with a waitress last weekend, following candlelight drinks on the terrace of his luxury New Forest hotel.

Ellie Brooks isn't Alek's usual type but the shapely waitress declared herself smitten by the workaholic tycoon, who told her he needed a vacation before his eye-wateringly bid deal. Seems the Greek tycoon takes relaxation quite seriously!

And, according to Ellie, Alek doesn't always live up to his Man of Steel nickname. "He's a pussycat", she purred. Perhaps business associates should keep a saucer of milk at the ready in future.

(35)

In this quotation, although this newspaper piece refers to his encounter with the heroine, the description of the hero (i.e. "the Midas touch billionaire" as well as the terms "workaholic tycoon", "Greek tycoon", and "Man of Steel") functions as indicators of his wealth, status, and corporate success. The aforementioned examples lead to the conclusion that the media is a powerful tool of the construction of the heroes' (celebrity) identity.

Based on the occasions and time periods, the media can paint someone black or white. As celebrity culture is heavily linked with fame, the media have the ability to idolise and exalt but also disparage and denigrate. In this case, elements such as wealth, power, and status seem to play a crucial role in the construction of the heroes' media representation and also (managerial) identity. What can be derived from the above is that the status of the heroes examined here is now linked with celebrity culture, and as such the celebrification that comes with it seems to reinforce heroes' transnational business masculinity.

Romance novels, as constituents of popular culture, seem to signpost a link between press and fame and the representation of the "Modern" hero. The male protagonist of these narratives is not just a very good looking man. Part of his heroic makeup is also that he is a celebrity. His "achieved" celebrification is the outcome of the hero's fruitful business accomplishments (and as a result his success, power and wealth) which, in turn, appear to portray the hero as an embodiment of transnational business masculinity.

In terms of the plot and love progression of the protagonists, fame (through press) serves multiple purposes in romance novels. Often, the press emphasises their attributes (wealth, status, power) and classes them as famous. On the other hand, on many occasions, it destroys the heroes' reputation and ruins their public image. Furthermore, it is this press vilification in the novels analysed here that triggers the hero to flee to the location where the first encounter with the heroine takes place. Ultimately, it is the driving force behind the quarrels and misunderstandings between the hero and heroine.

Overall, media is frequently presented as posing obstacles in the hero and heroine's emotional development and threatens the formation of a possible love relationship. But what it does, in combination with other elements, is paving the way towards a happily ever after ending. Furthermore, press and fame as well as cosmopolitanism (discussed below) appear to contribute to the formation of the heroes' managerial masculinity.

Cosmopolitanism and Attachment to Place

One of the most common characteristics of the "Modern" heroes discussed in this book is cosmopolitanism. According to Neil Lazarus, cosmopolitanism is the feeling of being "at home in the world". To be at home in the world is not only to be travelled and "worldly", it is to be capable of retaining one's centre of gravity, one's ability to be oneself, wherever in the world one might be" (Lazarus 2011: 119–20). John Tomaney defines cosmopolitanism as the "'global sense of place' with complete cultural openness" (Tomaney 2013: 662). Therefore, a cosmopolite is one who considers himself or herself a "citizen of the world". However, cosmopolitanism is a term with various connotations. Jonathan Ong (2009) suggests that there are four types of cosmopolitanism: "closed", "instrumental", "banal", and "ecstatic". "Closed" cosmopolitanism refers to a cosmopolitan individual who "reject[s] the ideal of openness" (454) and chooses to follow traditional discourses with regard to their identity. "Instrumental" cosmopolitanism describes a way of being that involves class and business and exhibits capital and luxury. In Ong's words, this type of cosmopolitanism is

> the most conscious mode of self-(re)presentation, as it is a social – and ultimately, *political* – performance of superiority which is hinged on a binary between the cosmopolitan and "the local". One is rich, the other poor. One is transient and mobile. The other is rooted and fixed. One enjoys limitless options. The other opts for the limits of locality.
> (456)

"Banal" cosmopolitanism is when one is in a way forced to associate with others (e.g. migrants in a foreign country). For Pnina Werbner, to be termed as "banal" cosmopolite, one "*inevitably must engage* with social processes of 'opening up to the world', even if that world is still relatively circumscribed culturally" (1999: 18). This process of becoming a cosmopolite is inevitable as it occurs when opening up to other cultures, social practices, and so forth. This type of cosmopolitanism is also termed as "ordinary" and "accidental" (Wright et al. 2013). Lastly, "'ecstatic' cosmopolitanism is the kind of cosmopolitanism that is passionately described in the media and morality literature" (Ong 2009: 460). This form of cosmopolitanism refers to the cosmopolitan, shared, and communal identity of people which is created by the media. It is related to "ecstatic news, an extraordinary class of news that manages to bring the globe together in the act of simultaneous watching" (Chouliaraki 2008: 378). In other words, it is the creation of a specific sense of togetherness through simultaneous watching of an event. All the diverse types of cosmopolitanism can be tied together as they are commonly characterised by "a willingness to engage with the other. It entails an intellectual and aesthetic openness towards divergent cultural experiences, a search for contrasts rather than uniformity" (Hannerz 1990: 239).

Taking these definitions and types of cosmopolitanism into account, most of the "Modern" post-millennial romance heroes that are examined here are depicted as "instrumental" cosmopolites. Cosmopolitanism seems to be a constituent of the transnational business masculinity that they embody. The heroes may reside in one place but their businesses operate in several. As Connell and Wood suggest, success in the corporate arena requires travelling internationally (2005: 356) and the adaptation of a life with "no more borders" for these businessmen (357). For example, Drakon Xanthis is a Greek man living in Naples while his businesses are located and operate in Southeast Asia. Nik, Leonidas, and Ludovic are of Greek origin but live and run their businesses from London. Nick (also Greek) is a classic car collector and auctioneer who lives and practices his profession in New York. However, it should be noted here that not all cosmopolitan businessmen are of Greek descent. For example, Rocco Modelli, featured in *The Italian's Deal for I Do* (Jennifer Hayward), is Italian and his is the "CEO of House of Modelli [. . .] a revered global couture powerhouse" (2015: 7), Chico Fernandez, in Susan Stephen's *In the Brazilian's Debt* (2015), is an infamous, Brazilian former polo player who now owns a world-class training ranch and the hero from *His Diamond of Convenience* (Maisey Yates 2015). Dmitri Markin is a Russian ex-martial arts fighter who owns a chain of gyms and a children's charity. The nationality of heroes is not of primary concern for the Harlequin and Mills & Boon publisher. Rather, apart from the international settings, what they seek is diversity: "the Mediterranean, Latin America, South East Asia, Africa [. . .] wherever he's from, it's certain that he turns the heads of every woman he passes! We love to see characters from a diverse range of backgrounds, cultures and experiences – it's all part of the international flavour of our books!"[4]

The internationality that is evident in the Harlequin and Mills & Boon "Modern" heroes examined here, and which is demanded for a successful corporate career, contributes to their cosmopolitan identities. These heroes can survive anywhere and identify themselves as part of a cosmopolitan community due to the mixture of cultures that they embody. The male characters of these romances embrace cultural differences, are well-acculturated, belong to the highest social class, and, due to the nature of their work, "display a luxurious capital" (Ong 2009: 456).

However, surprisingly, they also carry elements of "closed" cosmopolitanism. They have a sense of belonging and attachment to a place which contributes to the construction of their identity (Heidegger 1934). Here, place does not only refer to a geographical area. Rather, it signifies moments of social relations, experiences, and understandings (Massey 1991: 28). For bell hooks, this sense of belonging concerns "seeking a fidelity to a place" and "a vital sense of covenant and commitment" (hooks 2008: 65). The heroes mentioned earlier are international as they reside and operate globally. However, at the same time, their loyalty and attachment to their homeland remains close to their heart due to their past lived experiences and social relationships.

In *Petrakis's Power*, for example, Ludovic Petrakis is a cosmopolite who enjoys a luxurious life and capital. He is accustomed to travelling the world due to the nature of his businesses and appears to have adopted an international lifestyle, and, although he is a modern nomad, he is also represented as linked to a specific place. His mind always lingers on his family and the experiences they have shared. For Ludovic, Greece represents the family that he so quickly abandoned after his brother's death. No matter how hard he tries to detach himself from his place and the memories embedded in it, he does not succeed. The sense of belonging is deeply rooted in him. Now, the novel presents him as suddenly realising that he has been unfair to his family and it is time to return.

> He might have sought refuge in it when he'd exiled himself from his parents, but the exercise had failed miserably. All it had shown him was how emotionally barren his life had become. He was just kidding himself that he wanted to keep on travelling down the same soulless path. In truth, Ludo had missed his home and country much more than he'd realised.
>
> (*In Petrakis's Power* 2013: 120)

The hero has realised that is impossible to escape from the memories, from the past, and the elements that have constructed his personality and identity. It is these recollections that made him the man he is. Cosmopolitanism has tired him.

> It hit him now how tired he'd grown of endless travelling that filled most of his year. What he really wanted to do was to spend some proper time with family and friends, to immerse himself again in the simple

but solid values that shone like a beacon of goodness and common sense in a world where frequently moved too fast, where people restlessly went from one meaningless pleasure to the next in search of that most elusive goal of all [. . .] *happiness*.

(119)

In this quotation, cosmopolitanism is no longer seen as a desirable aspect in the hero's life. While once it was signalling a borderless world and the freedom of travelling, now (for the hero) it represents a complicated environment which isolates and prevents him from feeling at home and fulfilled. Conversely, his family and friends signify nostalgia and longing for an escape route out of the quickly advancing modern world. He appears ready to leave his cosmopolite nature behind, and seeks to re-embrace simplicity. He wants to reaffirm his sense of belonging and he finally achieves it when his father asks for the hero's forgiveness.

What matters is that you know I am proud of you and love you as deeply and strongly as I loved your dear brother. Can you forgive a very foolish old man for the stupidity of the past so that he may build a happier relationship with his beloved son in the future?

(168)

By accepting his father's apology, he rekindles his relationship with his father. The hero reinforces a link with the nucleus of his existence and feels "at home".

Nick, in *Greek for Beginners* (Braun 2013), is in a similar position to Ludovic's. The pursuit of his dream job has located him abroad with business all over the globe. He is a cosmopolite, transnational businessman who enjoys the privileges of capital and wealth. He is thrilled with his job, and although he loves his family, he chooses the cosmopolitan lifestyle

He loved his family. He loved Greece. But ever since he'd sold that first automobile to a collector living in the United States more than a decade earlier, he'd known that he would never settle for the quiet and predictable life he would have endured living here and working with his father.

(*Greek for Beginners* 2013: 36)

With properties in different places, and his demanding profession, travelling takes up a lot of his time. Despite his very successful and profitable career, Nick feels that his sense of belonging is fading away. He has not visited his homeland for a long time and his relationship with his family and brother is fragile as he feels betrayed by Pieter because of his wedding to Selene (the hero's ex-girlfriend). However, the novel emphasises that his family is always on his mind and an integral part of him. He now realises that he had "remained locked in his bitter disillusionment, isolated from his family, angry with the brother who had always been his best friend" (157). The novel suggests that without his past experiences and memories, he is incomplete and does not have a place to call home. Thus, he returns to Greece to attend the wedding. First, he must make amends with his brother "I hope I'm not too late to repair the damage my stubbornness has done. [. . .] If you still want me to act as your *koumbaro*, I would be honoured" (161). Pieter accepts the apology of his estranged brother and contributes to restoring the latter's sense of belonging. The place of the hero, his social relationships with family and friends, is now secured and with it so is his identity. For once again, in this novel too, the hero is shown as being a part of the location. The attachment to a place as well as cosmopolitanism is equally important for this hero. He has finally managed to balance his existence between home and the world. In both novels, the reaffirmation of the heroes' identity is achieved with the help of the heroines. They are the ones who make the heroes realise the importance of place in their lives.

Internationality is an attribute that partly reflects the heroes' transnational business masculinity, for to be a "'citizen of the world; [is] to reject immediately given and closed worlds of particularistic attachment" (Delanty 2006: 25). However, by bringing cosmopolitanism together with the attachment to a place, joining the global with the local, and linking the familiar (secure/safe environment, home) with the remote (unfamiliar, outside world), romance authors are trying "to reconcile tradition and modernity, topography and topology, home and world" (Tomaney 2013: 659).

Additionally, the fruitful mixture of place and local belonging gives the romance novel, and therefore the readers "a form of romanticized escapism from the real business of the world. While 'time' is equated with movement and progress, 'space'/'place' is equated with stasis and reaction" (Massey 1991: 26). For Ludovic "time" is London, while "space" signifies his home (and social/familial relationships) in Rhodes. Similarly, for Nick, Athens (and more importantly his family home) denotes escapism, a simpler way of life and stillness against pulsating Manhattan and a vibrant lifestyle. If cosmopolitanism represents the commotion of a globalised world, then place symbolises a welcoming diversion, that of tranquillity and serenity. One can suggest that the "Modern" heroes are not divided between local and global. Rather, they are represented as amalgamated identities constructed by tensions such as traditionality and modernity, distinctiveness and conformity, and locality and cosmopolitanism. The following chapter looks at the second form of masculinity that romance heroes employ.

Notes

1. As stated in the guidelines for prospective romance authors ("Write for Mills & Boon Modern") (www.millsandboon.co.uk/pages/write-for-modern-series).
2. The terms "managerial masculinity" and "transnational business masculinity" are used interchangeably by Connell.
3. "The barrier" is one of the eight essential elements Regis (2003) identifies in a romance novel and signifies the obstacles/reasons that may delay the unification of hero and heroine.
4. As stated on the publisher's website: www.millsandboon.co.uk/pages/write-for-modern-series.

Bibliography

Abrams, M. & Harpham, G. (2014) *A glossary of literary terms*. Stamford: Cengage Learning.

Allan, J. (2016) The purity of his maleness: masculinity in popular romance novels. *Journal of Men's Studies*, 24 (1), 24–41.

Ashton, L. (2012) *A girl less ordinary*. Richmond, Surrey: Harlequin Mills & Boon.

Boorstin, D. (1961) *The image: a guide to pseudo-events in America*. New York: Harper and Row.

Braun, J. (2013) *Greek for beginners*. Richmond, Surrey: Harlequin Mills & Boon.

Chouliaraki, L. (2008) The mediation of suffering and the vision of a cosmopolitan public. *Television & New Media*, 9 (5), 371–91.

Cohn, J. (1988) *Romance and the erotics of property: mass-market fiction for women*. Durham: Duke University Press.

Connell, R. ([1995] 2005) *Masculinities*. Cambridge: Polity Press.

——— & Wood, J. (2005) Globalization and business masculinities. *Men and Masculinities*, 7 (4), 347–64.

Cox, M. (2013) *In Petrakis's power*. Richmond, Surrey: Harlequin Mills & Boon.

Delanty, G. (2006) The cosmopolitan imagination: critical cosmopolitanism and social theory. *The British Journal of Sociology*, 57 (1), 25–47.

Drake, P. & Miah, A. (2010) The cultural politics of celebrity. *Cultural Politics*, 6 (1), 49–64.

Dyer, R. (1979) *Stars*. London: BFI.

Gilbert, S. & Gubar, S. (eds.) (2000) *The madwoman in the attic: the woman writer and the nineteenth-century literary imagination*. New Haven: Yale University Press.

Graham, L. (2000) *The Cozakis bride*. Richmond, Surrey: Harlequin Mills & Boon.

Hannerz, U. (1990) Cosmopolitans and locals in world culture. In Featherstone, M. (ed.) *Global culture: nationalism, globalization and modernity*. London: SAGE.

Hayward, J. (2015) *The Italian's deal for I do*. Richmond, Surrey: Harlequin Mills & Boon.

Heidegger, M. (1934) Why do I stay in the provinces? In Sheehan, T. (ed.) *Heidegger: the man and the thinker*. Chicago, IL: Precedent, 27–30.

hooks, B. (2008) *Belonging: a culture of place* [eBook]. New York and London: Routledge.

Jerslev, A. & Mortensen, M. (2016) What is the self in the celebrity selfie? Celebrification, phatic communication and performativity. *Celebrity Studies*, 7 (2), 249–63.

Kamblé, J. (2014) *Making meaning in popular romance fiction: an epistemology*. New York: Palgrave Macmillan.
Kendrick, S. (2013) *The Greek's marriage bargain*. Ontario: Harlequin Books S.A.
———. (2015) *Carrying the Greek's heir*. Richmond, Surrey: Harlequin Mills & Boon.
Kimmel, M. (1994) Masculinity as homophobia: fear, shame and silence in the construction of gender identity. In Brod, H. & Kaufman, M. (eds.) *Research on men and masculinities series: theorizing* masculinities. California: Sage, 119–41.
Krentz, J. (ed.) (1992) *Dangerous men and adventurous women*. Philadelphia: University of Pennsylvania Press.
Lazarus, N. (2011) Cosmopolitanism and the specificity of the local in world literature. *The Journal of Commonwealth Literature*, 46 (1), 119–37.
Lee, L. (2008) Guilty pleasures: reading romance novels as reworked fairy tales. *Marvels & Tales: Journal of Fairy-Tale Studies*, 22 (1), 52–66.
Massey, D. (1991) A global sense of place. *Marxism Today*, 38, 24–9.
Ong, J. (2009) The cosmopolitan continuum: locating cosmopolitanism in media and cultural studies. *Media Society Culture*, 31 (3), 449–66.
Penfold, R. (2004) The star's image, victimization and celebrity culture. *Punishment & Society*, 6 (3), 289–02.
Porter, J. (2013) *The fallen Greek bride*. Richmond, Surrey: Harlequin Mills & Boon.
Power, E. (2013) *A Greek escape*. Richmond, Surrey: Harlequin Mills & Boon.
Reagin, N. (2010) *Twilight & history*. New Jersey: John Wiley & Sons.
Rojek, C. (2001) *Celebrity*. London: Reaktion Books.
Stein, A. (2009) *The Byronic hero in film, fiction, and television*. Carbondale: Southern Illinois University Press.
Stephens, S. (2015) *In the Brazilian's debt*. Richmond, Surrey: Harlequin Mills & Boon.
Tomaney, J. (2013) Parochialism: a defence. *Progress in Human Geography*, 37 (5), 658–72.
Turner, G. (2010) *Ordinary people in the media: the demotic turn*. Los Angeles: Sage.
Urry, J. (2000) *Sociology beyond societies*. London: Routledge.
Werbner, P. (1999) Global pathways: working-class cosmopolitans and the creation of transnational ethnic worlds. *Social Anthropology*, 7 (1): 17–35.
Wright, D., Pyrhonen, S. & Heikkilä, R. (2013) Comparing "cosmopolitanism": taste, nation and global culture in Finland and the UK. *Comparative Sociology*, 12 (3), 330–60.
Yates, M. (2015) *His diamond of convenience*. Richmond, Surrey: Harlequin Mills & Boon.

3 Hybrid Masculine Bloc in Popular Romance Fiction

The term "hybrid masculine bloc"[1] was first introduced by Demetrakis Demetriou (2001: 348) in his critique of Connell's concept of hegemonic masculinity. Connell sees hegemonic masculinity as "always constructed in relation to various subordinate masculinities as well as in relation to women" (1987: 183). Demetriou refers to these two functions of hegemonic masculinity as "internal" and "external", respectively, and focuses on the former. He notes that Connell, by defining hegemonic masculinity as the social ascendancy of some men over others, creates a binary which places exemplary masculinities in opposition to counter-hegemonic masculinities. By doing so, Connell conceptualises hegemonic masculinities as "clearly demarcated from subordinated and marginalised ones" (Demetriou 2001: 346). In stark contrast, Demetriou posits that hegemonic masculinities do not exist "in tension with" (Connell 1993: 610) counter-hegemonic elements but rather they come together and construct a hybrid masculine bloc. The process of hybridisation – the ability of hegemonic masculinities to negotiate and appropriate elements from a variety of masculinities – makes hegemonic masculinity "the best possible strategy for the reproduction of patriarchy. That is, the configuration of practice that guarantees the reproduction of patriarchy need not necessarily be the one traditionally associated with white or heterosexual masculinities" (Demetriou 2001: 348). Taking Demetriou's notion on hybridity into account, this chapter will attempt to show that the twenty-first-century "Modern" heroes examined in the following sections are also embodiments of hybrid masculinity as they incorporate elements from counter-hegemonic masculinities while concurrently upholding their hegemonic status.

Emotional (In)accessibility

One of the established tropes in the romance narrative is the heroes' emotional inaccessibility (Frantz 2009). The heroes' inability to express their feelings

DOI: 10.4324/9781003202837-4

towards the heroines or others is part of their traditional, and old-fashioned, "hypertrophied" masculinity (Wendell and Tan 2009: 47). As Wendell and Tan suggest these heroes are "strong, dominating, confident men, often isolated" but also "hold a tortured, tender element within themselves that they rarely let anyone see" (77). It is only after the hero's association with the heroine (i.e. an already-established trope of the romance genre) that he is shown to incorporate counter-hegemonic elements and finally exhibit hybrid masculinity. Matters that trouble the heroes are resolved through the help of the heroines and the reciprocal nature of the protagonists' relationship. Although the heroes' help in most cases takes a financial form, the heroines' help is emotional. Often heroes are loners and estranged from their family. It is the heroine who reconnects them with their family and helps them make peace with their past.

For example, Ludovic Petrakis (*In Petrakis's Power*) is initially alienated from his family. When his brother dies in a sea accident close to Ludovic's private island, the hero travels abroad in haste and with a guilty conscience as he blames himself for the loss of his brother. Returning to make amends with his parents, and so going against the stereotypical masculine idea of not expressing emotions, he admits "I am their only son and heir. [. . .] I did not want to return until I could give them hope that the future was brighter than they had perhaps envisaged" (*In Petrakis's Power* 2013: 66). The once closed-off hero is now displaying his emotions and thoughts regarding his family to the heroine without fear of appearing feminine or weak:

> I discovered you can run away as far as you like – even to the remotest place on the planet – but you can't leave your sorrow and grief behind. Wherever you go, the pain travels with you. All running away did for me was add to my already unbearable sense of guilt and inadequacy. The realisation that as a son I had totally failed my parents – the people I love the most. They devoted their lives to raising me and Theo and look how I repaid them. It's unforgivable.
>
> (114)

However, at the beginning of the novel, he is presented as an emotionally repressed hero in need of the heroine's emotional support. Reluctant to face his parents alone, and afraid that he might disappoint them, he sees her as his way out of a difficult situation when he admits "Think of it as a harmless game of 'Let's Pretend'. Believe me when I say you are not hurting anybody" (73). To his parents and the hero, she is a bearer of hope and represents the beginning on a new, better future for the Petrakis's family. With her help and emotional support, Ludovic's relationship with his father is restored.

> There is nothing to forgive, Father. I too have made a grave mistake in believing that you didn't care for me as much as you did for my brother. I also have a stubborn streak and sometimes believe I am right when I am wrong.
>
> (168)

This example indicates that it is with the heroine's emotional support that the slow (re)configuration of hero's hegemonic masculinity takes place; through the appropriation of counter-hegemonic elements (in this case communicativeness) a hybrid masculinity – which encompasses a softer and emotional side of his character – is disclosed.

Similarly, in *The Darkest of Secrets* (Hewitt 2012), Khalis Tannous is estranged from his brother. The hero's estrangement is a result of his brother's illegal business practices which led to the death of their sister, Jamilah. Noteworthy features here are the heroine's actions which carry a reparatory sense and the notion of reciprocity that comes into play. Just as Khalis supported Grace during the trial for custody of her daughter, now it is her turn to help and "fix" him emotionally. The heroine supports him emotionally and forces him to build bridges between his past and future. She has given him an ultimatum: it is either the restoration of their relation or there will be no future with her.

> I'm saying [. . .] that if you can't even talk to your brother – your brother whom you thought was dead – then I can't be with you. I'm just stating facts, Khalis. Our relationship has been a mess of contradictions from the beginning. Keeping secrets even as we had this incredible connection. Amazing intimacy and terrible pain. Well, I don't want a relationship – a love – that is a contradiction. I want the real thing. Whole. Pure. Good.
>
> (*The Darkest of Secrets* 2012: 174)

Both Ludo and Khalis are represented as individuals tormented by memories, experiences, and social relations of the past. Their redemption comes only through the understanding and forgiveness of these situations that hold them back from their future. The starting point of their redemption is inherent in the emotional intervention of the heroines who function as catharsis and liberation from bonds of the past. If Khalis cannot forgive and welcome his brother back into his life, then he has not accepted his past and he has not forgiven himself. In this case, the heroine helps the hero make a successful transition from his past into his future. The hero's salvation is a prerequisite for the heroine's future. To ensure an emotionally prosperous future with the hero, the heroine has to first help him release himself from the past.

Contrary to the examples given earlier, where the heroines (at the start of the novels) are "forced" into a collaboration with the heroes, the heroine here takes the initiative herself. In this story, the hero (emotionally) needs the heroine because without her help and determination he has no future. At this section of the story, she represents everything that the hero lacks: willpower, emotional strength and decisiveness. Her personality trails are then acknowledged by the hero: *"you were right. I did need to face my past. Face my family. [. . .] I needed to forgive myself"* (184, emphasis added).

Another hero, Nick in *Greek for Beginners* (2013), has returned to Greece for his brother's marriage although the two of them are not on amicable terms as Pieter is marrying Nick's ex-girlfriend. Nick feels betrayed by his brother and refuses to give his blessing or become Pieter's best man. His single status prompts his mother and grandmother into matchmaking practices. To find a way out of this awkward situation, he asks the heroine to escort him to the wedding as his girlfriend: "I think we should keep it simple and as close to truthful as possible. I do not usually lie to my family" (*Greek for Beginners* 2013: 57). Not only does she agree to help him out and rescue him from the matchmaking and a potential bride, she also makes an effort to restore the close relation the two brothers once had. Her decisive emotional intervention is evident in the following quotation "you've held so tightly to the past, Nick, that you're robbing yourself of a future with your brother and the family you clearly adore" (157). Her emotional confidence, determination, and persistence make him behave more rationally. The fact that the heroine succeeds in reasoning with him seems to be important in the novel as he is made to acknowledge this and testify publicly that he needs more emotional help: *"you are right* [. . .] Darcie. I already have regrets where my brother is concerned. I do not want to have more" (158) (emphasis added). On this occasion (towards the end of the novel), the protagonists' roles have been reversed. The hero appears to have lost a part of his hegemonic nature. He lacks rationality and he needs the heroine's push to make a decision and act. It is the heroine who steers him out of trouble. She is considerate, understanding, and makes him realise what is important. She has also been attributed the traditionally feminine role of reminding the hero of the significance of the family. The hero admits that he needs her: "don't even think about backing out. I want you with me. *I* [. . .] *need you there*" (159, emphasis added). On the strength of the heroine's persuasion, Nick retrieves the love and close relation he had with his brother. Once again, the heroine has helped the two brothers re-establish their relationship and most importantly made the hero overcome his emotional barriers.

All three of the heroes mentioned earlier seem to share characteristics of hegemonic males: they are successful, possessing great wealth, authority, power, and exceptional beauty. Like most heroes, they have unsolved emotional concerns that the heroines help them overcome. What is striking here is the reversal of traditional gender roles between women and men. The heroines are no longer represented as weak and unprotected, rather, they are decisive and assertive. The heroes examined here require emotional rescue, a point antithetical to the traditional absence of emotionality in the construction of the heroes. These "Modern" heroes seem to encapsulate a form of hybrid masculinity; on one hand, they are pictured as strong and risk-taking fictional characters who appear to control and dominate the heroine financially or sexually or even both. On the other, they are shown to incorporate non-hegemonic elements and they are depicted "to have a softer side" (Vivanco 2012: 1065). It appears that in matters of the heart and emotions, heroes are weak and need guidance and advice. They hugely rely on the heroine to resolve their issues. Her role is crucial as she is the restorative link of a damaged and broken family. What is interesting here is the heroines' emphasis on men's emotionality and the former's function as an impetus towards the hybridisation of the latter or as Wendell and Tan put it, "whatever it is that tortures the hero, the heroine is key to his understanding and overcoming that flaw" (2009: 82). The heroes no longer typify the bourgeois masculinity as defined by David and Brannon who suggest that "masculinity depends on remaining calm and reliable in crisis, holding emotions in check. In fact, *proving you're a man depends on never showing your emotions at all.* Boys don't cry" (cited in Kimmel 1994: 125–6, emphasis added). On the contrary, as shown earlier, they seem to "openly and publicly embrace their emotional sides" without this making them seem unmanly (Salzman et al. 2006: 125) or lose part of their hegemonic status (Messner 1993: 731).

In the romance novels discussed here, one aspect that distinguishes this hybrid masculine bloc from traditional dominant masculinities is the heroes' ability to not only embrace their emotions but also control their sexual urges. The (sexual) self-restraint that the heroes demonstrate is discussed in the next section.

Self-restraint

Self-restraint is another convention of romance fiction that characterises the heroes' hybrid masculinity. These heroes display some characteristics of hegemonic masculinity – their glamour, wealth and success – but reject sexual domination as a way of gaining power over women. They are the men who do not hesitate to put their needs aside and control their sexuality. For them, the heroines and their emotions come first. As will be demonstrated further in the chapter, these heroes may sexually desire the heroine and may express their feelings for her; however, they do not actualise them.

Such a hero is Ludovic from *In Petrakis's Power*. He has everything: beauty, wealth, success, but he holds back sexually. He takes his time sexually provoking Natalie (i.e. touches, looks, innuendos), but he lets her take the initiative. For example, when she is shown to her bedroom in his house, the heroine asks whether they will be sharing it. The hero's reply carries a sexual innuendo:

> The only room you will share with me – and then only if you invite yourself- is *mine*. It is right next door to this one and the door will always be open during the night, should you feel inclined to visit me, *glykia mou*.
>
> (*In Petrakis's Power* 2013: 97–8)

This romance story is a continuous challenge and constant exchange of sexual comments between the hero and the heroine. This is evident in her response "as long as you don't take it for granted that I *will* visit you" (98) and his comment that follows: "Are you saying that you are not attracted to me?" (98) and "It is very gratifying that you can yield to temptation, *glykia mou* [. . .] because right now the temptation of *you* is sorely testing me" (111). Despite this electrifying and erotically intense atmosphere between them, the hero is sexually constraining himself: "He should give her time to realise that her own needs were just as great as his. When she came round to the fact of her own free will, the heat between them would be nothing less than *explosive*" (120). The hero makes a point of resisting his sexual urges and places importance on her feelings. Despite manoeuvring her into living in his house, he is patient and gives her time to realise and explore her feelings. He steps aside and allows her to be the initiator of a romantic relationship.

In a similar vein, Nick Costas's relationship with Darcie Hayes is based on mutual understanding but also a fiery sexual attraction (*Greek for Beginners*). He constantly shows her how much he yearns for a more intimate relation and so does she: "I will not claim to be a saint. A drink in your room poses too much temptation. [. . .] I am not coming in. [. . .] I want to picture where you will be sleeping tonight" (*Greek for Beginners* 2013: 90). Both the hero and heroine appear to torment themselves: they are flirting incessantly but without satisfying their sexual urges. When the heroine invites him to her hotel room, he yields to temptation for a moment. "His fingers fiddled at the nape of her neck. The knot in the bikini's halter went slack. [. . .] His hands moved lower, slowly exposing more of her skin inch by inch" but he soon restrains himself: "I can stop. I *should* stop" (136). What restrains him (sometimes more than the heroine) is the need for reassurance that both of them have the same feelings and are ready for this kind of commitment. In a sense, he needs the emotional guarantee that both of them are dedicated to make this work: "He wanted both of them going into in with eyes open and clear expectations. He didn't want the flash and burn of spontaneous sex. He wanted to make it last, make it count" (100). Therefore, seeing sexual intercourse as an act driven by passion – an act which could complicate things – and not reason, he refrains from it. What the hero wishes for is a long-lasting and strong relationship. To a certain extent, his choice contradicts the traditional hegemonic masculinity which is thought to seek "sexual conquest over women and separation from emotional involvement with them" (Holland 1993: 17), signifies the need for romance and companionship and points towards the emergence of his hybridity. Here the hero is torn between lust and emotions. Nevertheless, he chooses the latter over sexual activity. However, his actions do not lessen his dominant masculinity. Or as Connell puts it, "Hegemony does not mean total cultural dominance, the obliteration of alternatives". Rather, it is "achieved within a balance of forces, that is, a state of play" (Connell 1987: 184).

In *A Greek Escape* (Power 2013) the relationship between Kayla Young and Leonidas Vassalio is also overfilled with sexual signals and flirtation. What is different in this story is that although both of the protagonists are aware of their feelings, neither openly admits their desire for the other. Another established trope of the romance narrative is the heroine's sexual provocation (at times consciously and others unintentionally) which prompts a reaction from the hero and drives his self-control to its limits. For example, when he is repairing his car, she shows up wearing nothing but a "bikini with matching red and white wrap, which she tied, sarong-style, just above her breasts" (*A Greek Escape* 2013: 81) and asks if she can help him. Although both of them try to conceal the sexual attraction they feel for each other, they do not succeed: "do you think I would have achieved much with you looking like that?" (81) It is only then that she realises that she is actually "flaunting herself" (84). Despite his self-restraint and his attempt not to rush things, one incident at the beach makes him almost lose control. They kiss and he undresses her. Although she is lying naked in front of him, he finds the strength to fight his sexual needs and he does not penetrate her. Instead he gives her an orgasm. What stops this hero from penetrating and sharing the moment with her is his guilt for not revealing his true identity and mistakenly letting her believe he is only a builder. For him, sexual intercourse means commitment and commitment relies on honesty (an attitude to sexual intercourse which is often considered to be a traditionally feminine). Without being true to her, they cannot have a future together. To the hero's mind, honesty, as well as a mutual emotional involvement, is the foundation of a romantic relationship. Here, emotionality and the ability to understand and respect the heroine appear to be components of the hero's hybrid masculinity. The lack of dominance and bravado is replaced by sensibility and emotions (Salzman et al. 2006: 124).

Further support for the premise that the hero embodies a hybrid masculinity (i.e. has become more open to emotions and that he exercises self-control over his sexual desires) is Gabe Hollingworth in *First Time Lucky?* (Anderson 2012). He is a physiotherapist and Roxie Jones is a cheerleader. Both of them are involved with the same rugby team. Over the course of the novel, they battle each other with flirtatious expressions and sexual intimations. For the past five years, Roxie was acting as a carer for her late grandparents and did not have the opportunity to experience life like other teenagers. Now, her aim is to lose her virginity and have a sexual experience. The hero, on the other hand, restrains himself based on his belief that when a woman is sexually inexperienced and a virgin, emotions should be involved in a relationship's consummation. It is Roxie who makes the first move. As she is not interested in any sort of commitment and her attraction to the hero is purely sexual, she embarks on an exchange of sexual innuendos (based on lust) with him. For example, Roxie visits him for some treatment on her sprained ankle. While examining her he says "Spread your legs wider" (*First Time Lucky?* 2012: 40), but the heroine does not miss a chance to challenge him and replies "how wide?" (41). Later on, when she makes it clear that she wants him to be her first lover, he refuses. Through the use of innuendos, she attempts to provoke him sexually several times "You're not good enough as a lover?" (77), "You're so not the blaze I'd heard about" (78) and "Gabe, you know I want you to drive. [. . .] Just not my car" (91) but it proves fruitless. Regardless of her persistence and continuous flirting, he appears more sensitive, wise, and mature, and takes responsibility for her feelings when he suggests "you should want someone who's in love with you and who you're in love with" (74) but for her "the actual virginity bit is a mere practicality" (69). Here, his consideration and concern for her present a different form of masculinity: one that points towards hybridity. He appears to be more sensitive and considerate in contrast to the sexually liberated woman. Her sexual urges and persistence appear to be pushing the limits of his sexual restraint. Despite waking up and finding her in his bed, he does not give in to his sexual impulses and temporarily satisfies her needs by giving her an orgasm without entering her. His action signifies an awareness of her feelings and an attempt on his part to avoid emotionally hurting the heroine. Since he is not interested in commitment, he chooses to abstain from penetrative sex.

In summary, the Harlequin and Mills & Boon "Modern" hero of the chosen corpus presents a hybrid form of hegemonic masculinity. He may be burning with desire for the heroine but refrains from sexual intercourse and suppresses his urges in order to respect her and her feelings. A pattern emerges where the hero and heroine find themselves entwined in a "cat-and-mouse" game. This consists of constant (sexual) innuendos by both the protagonists and incomplete (sexual) acts until they mutually start developing feelings and reach the realisation that are in love with each other. What is noteworthy here is the (re)configuration of the heroes' masculinity. In stark contrast to Kimmel's view that "masculine identity is born in the renunciation of the feminine" (1994: 127), the heroes of these novels are depicted as understanding and patient and appear to value feelings and emotional commitment. Tragos described these men as "the new men" (2009: 544), strong, and sensitive. They embrace their "feminine side; [they are] enlightened enough to distinguish masculinity from machismo, and [accept their] new roles and behaviors as a badge in the service of gender democracy" (544). Moreover, they function as a means of reducing the hierarchical gap between the hero and heroine. Furthermore, the overtly sexual and more explicit behaviour of heroines acts as a counterpoise to the heroes' sexual restraint and the importance of commitment and love. As discussed here, traits such as self-restraint and emotional accessibility signpost the heroes' hybrid masculinity. The next chapter focuses on the elements of body and beauty which appear to be incorporated into all male protagonists of the aforementioned romance novels regardless of the form of masculinity they may embody.

Note

1. Demetriou's conceptualisation of the term "hybrid masculine bloc" has its roots in Antonio Gramsci's notion of historic bloc (1971: 59) and Homi Bhabha's concept of hybridity (1990: 221).

Bibliography

Anderson, N. (2012) *First time lucky?* Richmond, Surrey: Harlequin Mills & Boon.
Braun, J. (2013) *Greek for beginners*. Richmond, Surrey: Harlequin Mills & Boon.
Connell, R. (1987) *Gender and power: society, the person and sexual politics*. Sydney: Allen and Unwin.
———. (1993) The big picture: masculinities in recent world history. *Theory and Society*, 22, 597–23.
Cox, M. (2013) *In Petrakis's power*. Richmond, Surrey: Harlequin Mills & Boon.
Demetriou, D. (2001) Connell's concept of hegemonic masculinity: a critique. *Theory and Society*, 30, 337–61.
Frantz, S. (2009) Darcy's vampiric descendants: Austen's perfect romance hero and J. R. Ward's black dagger brotherhood. *Persuasions*, 30 (1). Available Online: www.jasna.org/persuasions/on-line/vol30no1/frantz.html
Hewitt, K. (2012) *The darkest of secrets*. Richmond, Surrey: Harlequin Mills & Boon.

Holland, J. (1993) *Sexuality and ethnicity: variations in young women's sexual knowledge and practice.* London: Tufnell Press.

Kimmel, M. (1994) Masculinity as homophobia: fear, shame and silence in the construction of gender identity. In Brod, H. & Kaufman, M. (eds.) *Research on men and masculinities series: theorizing* masculinities. California: Sage, 119–41.

Messner, M. (1993) "Changing men" and feminist politics in the United States. *Theory and Society,* 22 (5), 723–37.

Power, E. (2013) *A Greek escape.* Richmond, Surrey: Harlequin Mills & Boon.

Salzman, M., Matathia, I. & O'Reilly, A. (2006) *The future of men: the rise of the übersexual and what he means for marketing today.* New York and Hampshire: Palgrave Macmillan.

Tragos, P. (2009) Monster masculinity: honey, I'll be in the garage reasserting my manhood. *The Journal of Popular Culture,* 42 (3), 541–53.

Vivanco, L. (2012) Feminism and early twenty-first century Harlequin Mills & Boon romances. *The Journal of Popular Culture,* 45 (5), 1060–89.

Wendell, S. & Tan, C. (2009) *Beyond heaving bosoms: the smart bitches' guide to romance novels.* New York: Fireside.

4 Body and Beauty in Popular Romance Fiction

Popular culture and the mass media permeate everyday life and hold a dominant position in the social construction of standards and ideals. From magazines and newspapers to advertisements and television, individuals are being bombarded with new and updated forms of lifestyle, images, and gender. The influence exercised by these sources of entertainment and information is so great that it affects individuals' decisions on how to dress, act, and even how to project their sexuality. In this period, where success, prestige, and occupation partly depend on one's appearance and image, men and women seem to follow the trends that popular culture so endlessly produces. In other words, mass media not only influences people's thoughts of what is significant in the world but also guides their critical thinking and judgement about events and people (Kosicki 1993: 119). The information and knowledge that is conveyed to individuals from media is used as reference points and creates stereotypes. On the basis of these stereotypes, people evaluate what is socially acceptable and what is not (Iyengar 1991).

Romance fiction takes part in the same phenomenon as it presents ideal images for ordinary men and women to aspire to. To illustrate this point, the example of Jake from *A Girl Less Ordinary* is given. The hero of this novel finds himself under pressure to conform to the ideal image of masculinity reproduced by the mass media. He needs the heroine's support with his image (i.e. the way he presents himself). Although his managerial masculinity is one that could be described as dominant due to his business success and wealth, he is in need of a public relations analyst. When the sales of his smartphone company drop, the company's management board suggests the launch of a new campaign with the hero being the public face of the company. To reach this goal, they employ the heroine who is a rebranding and image consultant. Unlike most Harlequin and Mills & Boon heroes whose appearance reflects their status, Jake is

DOI: 10.4324/9781003202837-5

a walking "Before Picture". Hair that you don't cut often enough – and I'd guess that when you do you go to those "no need to book" salons [. . .] You're wearing a T-shirt that looks at least five years old, your jeans have a rip in them, and to say your shoes were scuffed would be kind.

(*A Girl less Ordinary* 2012: 39)

This quotation indicates the cultural pressure "modern men" are under to conform to images of idealised masculinity. Where once "fashion, grooming and the body [. . .] [were] more traditionally associated with women and femininity" (Edwards 2003: 143), now "masculinity is not a given, it is too created and manipulated through film, magazines, advertising and, of course, clothing" (Breward 1995: 216). Here, the heroine appears to assist the hero with having his traditional image of masculinity reworked to fit into modern society's standards of beauty and body.

For someone so wealthy and successful, Jake does not seem to have the slightest idea about personal appearance and the impact it makes in the corporate world. So, Ella is hired and with her professional and "personal brand" (*A Girl Less Ordinary* 2012: 38) advice, she attempts to put a face to the name everyone's heard of. Jake is reluctant to change and afraid of losing his individuality. He does not want to conform to the expected norm, and consequently in an attempt to keep his uniqueness, he resists Ella's suggestions about style, media, public appearances, and press interviews: "The navy blue suit and tie uniform, well, it made me feel like I'd been spat out the end of a Sydney businessman assembly line. [. . .] I felt homogenised, and I didn't like it" (104). While he is trying to stay away from publicity, Ella is listing the benefits of rebranding one's image:

> A person's image, and by that I mean their clothing, their grooming and their body language, has a massive impact on their lives. [. . .] It's about improving self-esteem and self-confidence – and even perceptions of capability or credibility. Re-evaluating your image can be life changing.
> (100)

The novel places the heroine in the argument around celebrity culture and rebranding and presents her as someone who is teaching the hero what he needs to know in order to maintain his company's success and improve his public image. The novel suggests that there is a clash between the inner self (i.e. identity) and appearance. Credibility, self-esteem, and self-confidence seem to contrast uniqueness and individuality. Therefore, the hero is worried that if he embraces the image (of masculinity) society is forcing upon him, he might lose part of his identity and self. It is only with the heroine's strong and professional views and her persistence in changing his appearance that the hero has to come around to admit that she was actually right: "Not at first, I'll admit. But you were right, last night. This whole image rebranding thing, it's been good for me" (170). Thanks to the heroine's determination, the campaign is a success, highlighted with interviews, conferences, and appearances at trade fairs. Ella not only saves the hero's company but has also taught him how to maintain a "good appearance" – one that reflected his managerial identity (as well as status and success) – be part of the upper-class social circle and survive the media scrutiny. The novel here refers to hegemonic masculinity (which is broadcast by the media) and its *changing* nature. What distinguishes the ideal man in the post-millennial romance novel from others in the past is that he is not only judged by his aggressiveness, risk taking skills, power, dominance, and wealth. The (public) image, appearance, and the way one carries the self are demonstrated as equally important elements that constitute part of one's identity. If "fashion satisfies a social need" (de Mooij 1998: 58) (to be socially accepted as member of a group) and "status is acquired by expressing either one's success or one's power and position in society" (59), then one may suggest that fashion creates an image which mirrors one's identity, success (achievements), and power, and reveals a certain status. Therefore, fashion can indeed be seen as a reflection of one's status. To conclude, the ideal dominant masculinity in many of these post-millennial "Modern" novels is not simply about having certain attributes. It is also about the recognition of importance and power, the presentation of one's self (and identity) and the perception of this image by others.

In recent decades, femininity has been under the microscope of mass media. An array of different ideas has constructed the ideal image (fashion and beauty) of the modern woman, the perfect body size and form, even behaviour. Jake's representation in this novel points out that over the past 20 years, the focus has shifted to masculinity. The "ideal body forms presented in Western media have changed over time, with declines in female body fat and increases in male muscularity" (Frederick et al. 2005: 84). Therefore, men find themselves under pressure to reaffirm their virility and manliness through muscularity as "it is still perceived as a cultural symbol of masculinity" (Elliott and Elliott 2005: 4). The majority of men now aspire to the idealised and mass media-constructed body shape; a muscular body "that has become an aesthetic norm for straights as well as gays" (Connell 1995: 185). The most desirable male body form for men and *women* (Olivardia et al. 2004; Pope et al. 2000) of the twenty-first century is of a "mesomorphic somatotype" (Elliott and Elliott 2005: 4). Therefore, the idealised male body form is a one characterised by a strong, muscular build and with "a well-developed chest and arms, with wide shoulders tapering down to a narrow waist" (Pope et al. 2000: 30).

In the context of romance fiction, it is rather unlikely to encounter a hero (whether transnational businessman, hybrid, or both) with an average body shape or form. The romantic hero's body often meets all the requirements to be considered as ideal. For example, Khalis Tannous has a "lean chest and lithe torso, muscled yet trim" and "he was beautiful, all burnished skin and sleek, powerful muscle" (*The Darkest of Secrets* 2012: 23–4). Travis Wilde is also "tall and long and lean and muscled. You could almost sense the hard delineation of muscle in his wide shoulders, and arms and chest, and she was almost certain he had a [. . .] six-pack" (*The Merciless Travis Wilde* 2013: 30). Gabe Hollingworth is a strong and muscular "broad-shouldered" hero with "the fit body, the tan, the muscles" (*First Time Lucky?* 2012: 15). In popular romance novels, muscularity goes hand in hand with sexual allure. The reason for this synergy lies in the modern construction of masculinity. As studies on masculinity have shown, due to mass media and its creation of the ideal image of male body, women in today's western societies are attracted more to men with a muscular body than others with an average build (Pope et al. 2000; Olivardia et al. 2004). If, based on today's ideals and standards constructed by the mass media, the ideal masculine body is muscular and muscularity equates to sexiness, then the more masculine the man is, the more intense the sexual allure.

The majority of Harlequin and Mills & Boon "Modern" line heroes examined here are described as attractive and masculine with an almost extravagant sexuality, which crosses the boundaries of realistically acceptable images to hyperbole. For example, Leonidas Vassalio is "lethally attractive" (*A Greek Escape* 2013: 25), "surprisingly hunky" with "black wavy hair and a strong jaw" (8), "thick winged brows" (9); and "thick ebony lashes framed eyes that were as black as jet and his brooding mouth was wide and form" (10). Beauty in romance narratives seems crucial as it equates to physical strength which, in turn, signifies masculinity (Cohn 1988: 155): "He was like a beautiful sleek stallion. All leanness and ripping muscle, with the power to dominate and excite, to control and to conquer using the pulsing energies and surging potency of his body" (*A Greek Escape* 2013: 82). Ludovic is described as: "a private viewing of the most sublime portrait by one of the great masters" (*In Petrakis's Power* 2013: 9). His physical features could constitute part of an artist's masterpiece. The portrayal of Nick's physical appearance is similar to the previously mentioned heroes. He is "six foot three [. . .] and every last inch of him [is] packaged in firm muscle. His hair [is] nearly black. The eyes below those brows [are] a rich chocolate-brown and smiling" (*Greek for Beginners* 2013: 11), "the man was built like a god, with ripped abs and the kind of chest that it seemed a sin to cover with a shirt" (133). In *The Cozakis Bride*, Nik Cozakis is described as beautiful but also dangerous and dark: "well over six feet [. . .]

the devastating dark good looks, the raw, earthly force of his sexual aura. All male. And those eyes, amber-gold as a jaguar cat, spectacularly noticeable in that lean, strong face" (*The Cozakis Bride* 2000: 18) and "exclusively sexy, intensively male" (89). These heroes are illustrated here as raw, virile, and strong alpha males whose beauty, sexuality, and manliness put them in a position "superior in degree to other men" (Frye 1957: 33).

What is interesting here is not so much the way that the heroes are pictured: beautiful, strong, muscular, sexy, and so forth. Rather, it is the emphasis and the excessive description of the body which becomes almost hyperbolic. Through the use of intended exaggeration, the body is given another dimension, is added more value, and is seen as the ultimate source of masculinity and virility. In many cases, the use of antiquity with historical references, mythology, and primitiveness seems to draw a portrait of heroes which also contributes to their excessive description and the construction of their beauty and hegemonic masculinity. Moreover, through the allusions to characters (usually gods) from the Greek mythology, the heroes seem to receive an ideal beauty far greater than the rest of the men and equal to the beauty of a god. The "process of idealisation" is common for romance authors as they use it as a technique to "highlight similarities between their own protagonists and well-known figures from myths" (Vivanco 2011: 69). Ludovic and Nick, for example, are described in terms of the Greek mythic gods: "the chiselled good looks of a modern-day Adonis" (*A Greek Escape* 2013: 10) and "as handsome as Adonis" (*Greek for Beginners* 2013: 39), respectively. Adonis, in Greek mythology, was the lover of goddess Aphrodite and the mythological archetype of beauty and desire.

In addition to the physical perfection, and taking into account that the story is recounted from the heroines' point of view, the comparison to Greek gods hints at the intensity of their (heroines') sexual desire for the heroes (Vivanco 2011: 70). The following quotation describes the way the heroine views the hero. Leonidas is incredibly sexy and when he says the heroine's name, "her name dripped from his lips like ambrosia from the lips of Eros, although she doubted that even the Greek god of love could have harboured the degree of sensuality this man possessed" (*A Greek Escape* 2013: 58). Leonidas's association with the mythical god Eros reinforces his sensuality and makes him "superior *in degree* to other men" (Frye 1957: 33). He exemplifies Frye's high-mimetic hero: he has "passions and powers of expression far greater than ours" (1957: 34). To conclude, the heroes' beauty is seen as extraordinary or a masterpiece in an attempt of the authors to emphasise their appearance and indicate the heroines' sexual attraction for the heroes.

The intended exaggeration of the ideal (muscular) body along with the references to Greek mythology indicates a link with the development of body culture in ancient Greece. In Stewart's words, in ancient Greece, "the male body was a specific metaphysic of masculinity, of masculine presence as such" which now in western culture "operates as a standard against [. . .] less well-formed bodies" (1997: 67). What derives from this section is that muscularity, sexuality, and manliness are entangled characteristics of the romance hero. They constitute an important part in the development of the protagonists' sexual relationship as they are the first characteristics to be noticed.

There are several reasons why romance heroes are excitingly muscular and sexually appealing. In both ancient Greece and Renaissance periods, muscularity became a requisite for the ideal body through statues of gods and heroes (Varanese 2013). This strong and muscular body image has survived through the ages and today it has been adapted and used by the media (Leit et al. 2002). In their study, Kjelsås et al. (2004) suggest that the media propagates and reinforces perceptions about the body. These perceptions differ for men and women, the latter striving to achieve thinness, the former aiming for muscularity (Cash and Brown 1989; Ridgeway and Tylka 2005). In this modern era, romance fiction is reinforcing the male body form constructed by the mass media. Furthermore, romance is a fiction genre written mainly for women by women and the romance novel is a fictitious story offering women a glimpse of the unachievable, the fantasy for a utopian male body, their secret desire and wish to identify with the heroine, and have (fictitiously and for a short period of time) an ideal masculine hero sexually caressing them. The focus on masculinity through body shape highlights the important position that sex and the eroticisation (especially of men) hold in the post-millennial popular romance novels examined here.

Bibliography

Anderson, N. (2012) *First time lucky?* Richmond, Surrey: Harlequin Mills & Boon.
Ashton, L. (2012) *A girl less ordinary.* Richmond, Surrey: Harlequin Mills & Boon.
Braun, J. (2013) *Greek for beginners.* Richmond, Surrey: Harlequin Mills & Boon.
Breward, C. (1995) *The culture of fashion.* Manchester and New York: Manchester University Press.
Cash, T. & Brown, T. (1989) Gender and body images: stereotypes and realities. *Sex Roles*, 21, 361–73.
Connell, R. ([1995] 2005) *Masculinities.* Cambridge: Polity Press.
Cox, M. (2013) *In Petrakis's power.* Richmond, Surrey: Harlequin Mills & Boon.
de Mooij, M. (1998) Masculinity/femininity and consumer behaviour. In Hofstede, G. (ed.) *Masculinity and femininity: the taboo dimension of national cultures.* London and New Delhi: Sage, 55–76.
Edwards, T. (2003) Sex, booze and fags: masculinity, style and men's magazines. *The Sociological Review*, 51 (1), 132–46.

Elliott, R. & Elliott, C. (2005) Idealized images of the male body in advertising: a reader-response exploration. *Journal of Marketing Communications*, 11 (1), 3–19.
Frederick, D., Fessler, D. & Haselton, M. (2005) Do representations of male muscularity differ in men's and women's magazines? *Body Image*, 2, 81–6.
Frye, N. (1957) *Anatomy of criticism: four essays*. Princeton: Princeton University Press.
Graham, L. (2000) *The Cozakis bride*. Richmond, Surrey: Harlequin Mills & Boon.
Hewitt, K. (2012) *The darkest of secrets*. Richmond, Surrey: Harlequin Mills & Boon.
Iyengar, S. (1991) *Is anyone responsible? How television frames political issues*. Chicago: University of Chicago Press.
Kjelsås, E., Bjørnstrøm, C. & Götestam, K. (2004) Prevalence of eating disorders in female and male adolescents (14–15 years). *Eating Behaviors*, 5, 13–25.
Kosicki, G. (1993) Problems and opportunities in agenda-setting research. *Journal of Communication*, 43, 100–27.
Leit, R., Gray, J. & Pope, H. (2002) The media's representation of the ideal male body: a cause for muscle dysmorphia? *International Journal of Eating Disorders*, 31 (3), 334–8.
Marton, S. (2013) *The merciless Travis Wilde*. Richmond, Surrey: Harlequin Mills & Boon.
Olivardia, R., Pope, H., Borowiecki, J. & Cohane, G. (2004) Biceps and body image: the relationship between muscularity and self-esteem, depression, and eating disorder symptoms. *Psychology of Men and Masculinity*, 5, 112–20.
Pope, H., Phillips, K. & Olivardia, R. (2000) *The Adonis complex: the secret crisis of male body obsession*. New York: Free Press.
Power, E. (2013) *A Greek escape*. Richmond, Surrey: Harlequin Mills & Boon.
Ridgeway, R. & Tylka, T. (2005) College men's perceptions of ideal body composition and shape. *Psychology of Men and Masculinity*, 6, 209–20.
Stewart, A. (1997) *Art, desire and the body in ancient Greece*. Cambridge: Cambridge University Press.
Varanese, J. (2013) Social construction of deviance: male body image. *Sociological Imagination: Western's Undergraduate Sociology Student Journal*, 2 (1).
Vivanco, L. (2011) *For love and money: the literary art of the mills & boon romance*. Penrith: HEB.

5 "Lesser" Masculinities

In the twenty-first-century romance novels, the heroes and heroines still remain the main protagonists. However, they do not monopolise the romance story. Other characters and lesser masculinities have always existed in the romance stories and formed sub-stories enriching the hero or heroine's past and familial or work environment. They sometimes were the trigger for the two protagonists to meet and approach each other.

The authors of the post-millennium novels in the chosen corpus discuss these failed lovers and reveal traits of their personality, character, authority, and power. However, the amount of information given is no more than what is deemed "necessary to provide background for the main storyline" (Ramsdell 2012: 50). Tad in *Greek for Beginners* is an example of a failed lover; he is the heroine's ex-fiancé. Throughout the novel, he is described as a penny-pinching man who is unwilling to spend any money for their honeymoon: "Tad has never earned a penny that he hadn't pinched mercilessly afterward" (*Greek for Beginners* 2013: 9). He is also pictured as someone who is overly attached to his mother: "The last draw was when Tad started talking about adding another master suite on to her [his mother's] house instead of continuing to look for a house of our own after we got married" (87). He is not portrayed as romantic. Rather, "Tad wasn't one to give compliments. Even during the courtship phase of their relationship, pretty words had been few and far between" (23). Avoiding commitment, Tad is hesitant and unwilling to take things further with Darcie and introduce her to his family "She'd dated Tad more than a year before he'd taken her home to meet his mother" (45).

As an egotistical man who wants to maintain superiority over his wife, Tad is not encouraging Darcie to follow her dream career: "A journalism career, especially one that eventually might take her to New York, wasn't in his cards for his future wife" (102). Darcie is neither the centre of his world, nor part of his plans. He is more interested in himself, his career, and his mother.

DOI: 10.4324/9781003202837-6

Overall, the purpose of Tad's literary existence in the novel is threefold: first, he constitutes part of the heroine's life and therefore provides the reader with an overview of her past experiences. Second, he justifies her decision to leave him behind, and most importantly, thirdly, he functions as a foil for the hero. Nick Costas, the hero, is described as everything Tad is not. The latter is the foundation onto which the main hero's attributes and character are created. The failed lover is the unsatisfying and incomplete state of the male protagonist of the story.

Another man who is compared unfavourably to the hero in *A Greek Escape* is Craig Lymington, the heroine's ex-fiancé. He is portrayed as an unfaithful and shallow man: "that night when she discovered those messages on his cell phone and realised that she wasn't the only woman to whom he'd whispered such hollow and meaningless words" (*A Greek Escape* 2013: 14). He is an immoral man who feels no shame as he is marrying somebody else (one of the heroine's colleagues) on the day he was supposed to marry the heroine: "He just kept the same date and the same time at the same church with the same photographer for *convenience*" (55). He is also anti-social, his life is limited to his job – "He didn't have any real friends. They were all company people. People he'd met through his job. Sales reps. Customers. His management team and their wives. The office hierarchy that he liked [. . .] to socialise with" (56) – and an overly ambitious man solely concerned about his career and his professional progress and development:

> Accompanying Craig to company dinners and luxury conference weekends where she had watched her ex paying homage [. . .] to people he merely wanted to impress – people he knew could further his corporate ambitions – without really liking them at all.
>
> (42)

This failed hero shares common characteristics with the main male protagonist of the novel. He is successful, ambitious, and with a vision of climbing the ladder of corporate hierarchy, but, in contrast to the main hero, he lacks in feelings. Leonidas Vassalio, the main hero of the story, is eager to get the heroine's attention; he is flirtatious with her and emotionally approaches her.

What differentiates this failed lover is his lack of interest and emotions for the heroine. Her presence in his life is not important as she solely functions as a boost for his image and ego. His occupation is of great importance to him and has never allowed for balance between work and family time. His ego and male chauvinism result from such a prosperous profession: "The type with a nicely pressed suit and a spare clean shirt in the office closet. The type who's always late home because his workload's so heavy.

The type who thinks every reasonably attractive female colleague is only there to boost his ego" (56). In this novel, being a businessman is rendered as a terrible occupation. What the heroine finds abhorrent in businessmen is their dedication to work and nonchalant attitude towards their private life. She is surprised by their ruthlessness in order to achieve what they want without considering the effects their actions may have on others, as well as the presentation of their masculinity as superior to femininity. These businessmen see women as inferior and only useful in assisting them in achieving their goals and boosting their egos.

Generally, this character is described as selfish, unfaithful, with no moral barriers, and with the intention to professionally succeed at all costs. Similar to Tad, Craig's common masculinity is set as a foundation for constructing a hero superior and better in kind (i.e. Leonidas). The former masculinity is subordinate with regard to the idea that hegemonic masculinity in romance novels is about not being sexist, not mistreating women, but treating them as equals and understanding that the beloved should be at the centre of their lives. Although the failed hero embodies good qualities, they only encompass the corporate world. His attributes do not fulfil the heroine's emotional demands. The latter, on the other hand, is the embodiment of her wishes. He is the ideal partner, a successful, wealthy hegemonic male who can also fulfil her emotional needs and wishes. To the heroine, Craig and Leonidas form the two opposite poles on a sliding scale of masculinity. What differentiates the two male heroes is their level of emotionality, understanding, and companionship.

Rupert Henshawe in *Mistletoe and the Lost Stiletto* (Fielding 2010) is a ruthless businessman with no morals who uses the heroine Lucy to launch his new chain of fashion retail stores. He has everything planned. He pretends he is in love with the heroine and she is left to plan their wedding only to discover that the romance they shared was a well-organised marketing campaign. She had been carefully selected to represent his new business endeavour due "to her enthusiasm, her natural openness and lack of guile" (*Mistletoe and the Lost Stiletto* 2010: 47) He made her the new face to launch his campaign as

> he wanted a real woman who [*sic*] he would transform with his new "look". An ordinary woman. [. . .] Not a model or a star, but someone who every women in their sales demographic would instantly relate to, aspire to be. Would believe.
>
> (84)

Rupert does not hesitate to manipulate and take advantage of the heroine. Not only is he not considerate of her feelings but he also unashamedly uses her for financial gain and the expansion of his business empire. He is shown as heartless and with a sole interest in his wealth. In order to achieve his ingenious plans, he carefully chooses his marionette based on her background: she was abandoned as a baby, grew up in several foster homes, with no education or family to care for her. Once he has no use of her, their relationship will be over:

> The breakup scenario is already written, by the way. [. . .] Apparently, I'm going to call off the wedding because Rupert is a workaholic, too absorbed in business to spend time with me. True, as it happens. Sadness, but no recriminations. Nothing sordid. Just a quite fade out of the relationship once the stores are open and the brand established.
> (150)

In general, the author of this romance story, in an attempt to reinforce Nathaniel's masculine attributes, draws Rupert as a ruthless businessman, eager to increase his wealth at the expense of the heroine's feelings. He is not interested in the emotional damage caused. He is temporarily selling her the kind of life she is dreaming of only for his benefit and functions as an utter contradiction to the hero's character. By diminishing Rupert, Nathaniel is almost simultaneously placed on the pedestal for his virtuous and noble qualities.

To conclude, these are some examples of the men who receive a place in the romance story along with the main protagonists. At times, and depending on the story, they are given integral positions and roles in order to help the love progression of the hero and the heroine, while on other occasions, they just remain in the background and are only used as references of the past. Whatever position they hold, they act as catalysts and bring the hero and heroine together. Additionally, they embody the "before" of a better "after", an inadequate and poor projection of masculinity and a failed lover inferior to the masculine main hero. They are purposely pictured as such, and function as enhancements of hegemonic masculinities in romance novels.

Bibliography

Braun, J. (2013) *Greek for beginners*. Richmond, Surrey: Harlequin Mills & Boon.
Fielding, L. (2010) *Mistletoe and the lost stiletto*. Richmond, Surrey: Harlequin Mills & Boon.
Power, E. (2013) *A Greek escape*. Richmond, Surrey: Harlequin Mills & Boon.
Ramsdell, K. (2012) *Romance fiction: a guide to the genre*. California: Libraries Unlimited.

Conclusion

Hegemonic masculinity is the recognition of a particular image of masculinity as superior to other masculinities and femininities. It is a socially constructed unattainable notion which depends, amongst other factors, on time period, culture, and location. The "Modern" heroes examined here are pictured as characters that embody different forms of dominant masculinity. They are depicted to personify transnational business masculinity; they are self-centred, ruthless, powerful, wealthy, authoritative, and self-serving businessmen. These individuals are eager to increase their assets, maximise their profit, and do anything in their power to reach their aims, actualise their goals, and derive pleasure. Occasionally, they might use their wealth, capital, and power to take advantage of the heroine in need to reach their goals. Nevertheless, once they fall in love and propose some kind of betrothal, their dominant position starts to crumble. Similarly to novels in the past, the heroes' wish for a shared life with the heroine offers her power, access to their wealth, capital, and luxury as well as rise in social class and status. Also, they often present hybrid masculinity or, as Salzman et al. put it, a "lite" version of masculinity – one that emphasises sensibility and sensuality over power and bravado (Salzman et al. 2006: 124). However, it should be noted here that the incorporation of elements from these two forms of masculinities does not necessarily imply the negation of one (form of dominant masculinity) by the other, or their interdependence.

Cosmopolitanism is a characteristic that "Modern" heroes share and one that seems to constitute part of their image as transnational business masculinities. These heroes are cosmopolites with global business activities and constant travelling. They are multifaceted identities as they are constructed from "instrumental" and "closed" cosmopolitanism. They embody a complete cultural openness, they are comfortable in any foreign location, and they enjoy the glamour of travel, of spanning the world. They have links and connections with the rich all over the world, and live and consume in luxurious manner. However, at the same time, they are attached to a place (through memories, social relationships, past, and lived experiences), pursue, and value simplicity. They have a sense and confidence of belonging which distinguishes them from the rest of the masculinities. Cosmopolitanism and parochialism exist in balance in the heroes. Where cosmopolitanism represents the modern, relentlessly evolving world, their attachment to a place (home/homeland/family) for them is nostalgia – of something lost and re-found with the help of the heroine – tradition, a sense of solace, tranquillity, and escapism to a more relaxed environment/location.

Another mutual feature of these "Modern" heroes is their association with press and fame. As celebrities, their fame is both "acquired" and "attributed". However, the fame they receive, whether it is due to their achievements as businessmen or their "well-knownness", is linked with, and makes references to, elements such as wealth, power, status, and position in the corporate arena; it appears to first and foremost reinforce their image as transnational business masculinities. Moreover, in some novels, (negative) press and fame also trigger the hero to flee to the place where his first encounter with the heroine takes place.

The second form of dominant masculinity that the heroes typify, that of hybridity, becomes apparent through the heroes' acknowledgement and (open) expression of their feelings. In the beginning of the romance stories, these "Modern" heroes are featured as emotionally inaccessible and estranged from their family. The heroine's persistence, understanding, and, sometimes, advice help them overcome emotional issues and restore their relationship with their family. It is with her help and persistence that the heroes are gradually introduced to hybridity and begin to open up emotionally. Moreover, during their encounters with the heroines, the heroes are also characterised by self-restraint. Although both protagonists participate in a constant exchange of sexual innuendos, the heroes appear reluctant to make the first move towards the sexual intercourse. For them, sex comes with emotional intimacy and commitment and it is their priority to ensure that mutual feelings are shared. They are sensitive, take into account the heroine's feelings, and place them above their sexual urges. They are men who are incorporating

> this new masculinity [and are aware] that caring for themselves extends their capacity to care for others – their female partners, male friends, extended family. [. . .] And they understand that caring for the whole range of beings who contribute to their emotional lives isn't "womanish" or "unmanly".
>
> (Salzman et al. 2006: 210)

Regardless of the form of masculinity, the aforementioned heroes exemplify, the ideal body form is that of increased muscularity. In the chosen romance novels, the body goes hand in hand with muscularity and sexual allure. Therefore, the more muscular the body is the more masculine and sexual alluring the hero. The muscularity that romance writers employ reinforces the stereotype of the dominant masculine body. Furthermore, these authors offer the female readership the temporary excitement of fictitiously living the unattainable. Moreover, although not a recent theme, this given emphasis on the body highlights the crucial position that eroticism and sex still hold in the popular romance narratives of my corpus.

Another way that romance novels preserve hegemonic masculinity (of any form) is through other, lesser masculinities. Although the love relationship occupies the largest part of the narrative, it does not monopolise it. Other men and women exist and form sub-stories. These sub-stories provide information regarding the hero and heroine's past and background. At times, they also contribute to the first encounter of the protagonists. Furthermore, they function as comparisons to the protagonists. It appears that, by devaluing them, the authors simultaneously exalt the protagonists.

Overall, the popularity of romance fiction derives from the genre's ability to adapt to different time periods, social changes, and phenomena. By drawing from this discussion, the romance hero appears to be a complex construction: he carries hypermasculine traits, such as wealth, strength, assertiveness, and an ability to lead, elements that point towards, and support, his transnational business masculinity. But he also embraces and demonstrates hybrid masculinity. He is flexible, understanding, and considerate. He embraces his emotions and exhibits (sexual) self-restraint. His qualities (hegemonic and counter-hegemonic) do not clash with each other but rather coexist and form an image of a more realistic man. After all, "The definition of the Real Man is that in today's culture, he is expected to be flawed, or at least to show some kind of vulnerability" (Salzman et al. 2006: 61). Taking this definition under consideration, the hero examined here is not a construction of a novel masculinity. Rather, he is an embodiment of different forms of dominant masculinities which can be seen as both a revision and a continuation of the hegemonic masculinity portrayed in romance novels.

Bibliography

Salzman, M., Matathia, I. & O'Reilly, A. (2006) *The future of men: the rise of the übersexual and what he means for marketing today*. New York and Hampshire: Palgrave Macmillan.

Index

Abrams, M.H. 27
achieved celebrity 32, 34
action/adventure stories 5
Adonis 57
Allen, Eric 7
alpha male 19, 57
Amazon 8
American Marketing Association 2
Anderson, Natalie 50
animal behaviour 19
anti-hero 27
Aphrodite 57
ascribed celebrity 32
Ashton, Leah 33
attachment 38–40
attributed celebrity 32, 34–5

banal cosmopolitanism 36
Barthel, Diane 21
beauty 53–8
Beckham, David 21
belonging 38–40
body image/shape 53–8, 65–6
Bourdieu, Pierre 1
bourgeois masculinity 47
branding 2, 8
Braun, Jackie 39
Brazilian's Debt (Stephen) 37
Buerkle, C. Wesley 21
Byrd, Rhyannon 8
Byronic hero 27

Carrigan, Tim 18
Carrying the Greek's Heir (Kendrick) 25, 34–5
celebrification 31–2

celebrity culture 31–5, 54–5, 65
Chatsfield, The 9
Christian fiction 4, 7
closed cosmopolitanism 36, 38
Clow, Kimberley A. 21
Cohn, Jan 2
Collins, Dani 11
Connell, Raewyn 12, 18, 25–7, 37, 43, 49
Contemporary Romance 10–11
Cooper, Tim 6, 7
cosmopolitanism 36–40, 64–5
counter-hegemonic masculinity 43
Cox, Maggie 26
Cozakis Bride, The (Graham) 26, 28, 56–7

Darkest of Secrets, The (Hewitt) 45, 56
Dark Wolf Returning (Byrd) 8
Demetriou, Demetrakis 12, 43
Desire series 5
DiCaprio, Leonardo 18
digital reading applications 6–7
dominant masculinity 18–19, 22, 25–6, 65–6
Donaldson, Mike 18

eBooks 5, 6–7
ecstatic cosmopolitanism 36–7
emotional inaccessibility 43–7, 65
Enderlin, Jennifer 8
Eros 57
erotica 5

failed heroes/lovers 60–3
Fallen Greek Bride (Porter) 26, 29

fame 31–6, 65
Faulds, David 8
femininity 21, 51, 53–4, 55
fictional modes 19–20, 57
Fielding, Liz 62
Fifty Shades of Grey (James) 5
First Time Lucky? (Anderson) 50, 56
Fjermestad, Jerry 7
Flesch, Juliet 11
Flood, Alison 5
For Love and Money (Vivanco) 19
Frantz, Sarah 11
Friends (Bassett and Vance) 5
Frye, Northrop 19–20, 57

Gelder, Ken 1
gender roles 47
Gilbert, Sandra 27
Girl Less Ordinary, A (Ashton) 33–4, 53
Glossary of Literary Terms (Abrams and Harpham) 27
Graham, Lynne 26
Greek Escape, A (Power) 32, 49, 56, 57, 61
Greek for Beginners (Braun) 39–40, 46, 56, 57, 60
Greek mythology 57–8
Greek's Marriage Bargain, The (Kendrick) 26, 29–30
Guardian, The (newspaper) 5, 6
Gubar, Susan 27

Harlequin 2–9, 37
Harlequin Flipside 4–5
Harlequin Heartwarming 7
Harlequin Historical 7
Harlequin Medical Romance 7
Harlequin Presents 7, 11
Harlequin Reader Service 3
Harpham, Geoffrey 27
Hayes, Donna 4–5
Hayward, Jennifer 37
Hearn, Jeff 18
hegemonic heterosexual masculinity 18
hegemonic masculinity 12, 17–22, 43, 46–51, 57, 62–3, 64, 66
hegemony 12, 17–18, 49
Heisey, Lawrence 2
heroes 12, 17–22, 26–31, 33–5, 38–40

heroines 5, 10, 11, 20, 22, 25, 27–31, 33–6, 40, 44–51, 53–5, 57, 58, 60–6
Hewitt, Kate 45
high-mimetic mode 20, 57
His Diamond of Convenience (Yates) 37
hybrid masculinity 12, 22, 43–51, 64, 65, 66
hypermasculinity 21–2
hypertrophied masculinity 44

idealised masculinity 53–8
instrumental cosmopolitanism 36
International Association for the Study of Popular Romance, The 11
internationality 37, 40
ironic mode 20
iron-man surfing champion 18
Italian's Deal for I Do, The (Hayward) 37

James, E.L. 5

Kamblé, Jayashree 26
Kendrick, Sharon 25, 26
Kjelsås, Einar 58

Lazarus, Neil 36
lesser masculinities 12, 60–3
Love Inspired series 7
low-mimetic mode 20

male hegemony 18
managerial masculinity *see* transnational business masculinity
manga 4
Mangold, Glynn 8
Markert, John 3
marketing 2–3, 6–9
masculinity: bourgeois masculinity 47; concept 10; counter-hegemonic masculinity 43; dominant masculinity 18–19, 22, 25–6, 65–6; feminine 21, 51, 54; hegemonic masculinity 12, 17–22, 43, 46–51, 57, 62–3, 64, 66; hybrid masculinity 12, 22, 43–51, 64, 65, 66; hypermasculinity 21–2; hypertrophied masculinity 44; idealised masculinity 53–8; lesser masculinities 12, 60–3, 66;

Index

subordinate masculinity 43, 62; transnational business masculinity 12, 22, 25–40, 56, 64–6
McCracken, Scott 1–2
media 31–6, 53–4, 58, 65
Merciless Travis Wilde, The (Marton) 56
mesomorphic somatotype 55
Messerschmidt, James 18
metrosexuality 21
Meyer, Stephenie 5
Mills & Boon 1–9, 37
Mira Books 5
Mistletoe and the Lost Stiletto (Fielding) 62–3
Modern series 11, 12
muscularity 55–8, 65–6
mythic mode 20

Netflix 8
Nocturne series 5, 20
nonfiction 5

Ong, Jonathan 36–7

paranormal stories 5, 20
parochialism 65
patriarchy 21, 43
Petrakis's Power, In (Cox) 25, 26, 27–8, 38, 48, 56
Pittman, Frank 21
Porter, Jane 26
poststructuralism 10
Power, Elizabeth 32–4, 49
Publisher's Weekly (trade news magazine) 5

Regis, Pamela 11
Ricciardelli, Rosemary 21
rogue heroes 27, 30
Rojek, Chris 32
Romance Reading Challenge 8
Romance Writers of America 11

romantic mode 20
Rose of Romance Book Club 9

Salzman, Marian 64
Schell, Heather 19
self-restraint 47–51, 65, 66
Sensual Romance series 5
sexuality 19, 21, 27, 47–9, 51, 53, 56–8, 65–6
Silhouette Bombshell series 5
Silhouette Sensation series 5
Simpson, Mark 21
social media 8, 9
Steeple Hill Books 5
Stephen, Susan 37
stereotypes 21, 44, 53–4, 65–6
Stewart, Andrew 58
St. Martin's Press 8
subgenre 10–11
subordinate masculinity 43, 62

taboos 10–11
Talbot, Mary 19
Tan, Candy 47
Thomas, Glen 2
Tomaney, John 36
transnational business masculinity 12, 22, 25–40, 56, 64–6
Tyson, Mike 18

Ultimate Seduction, The (Collins) 11

Vivanco, Laura 11, 19–20

Wayne, John 18
Wendell, Sarah 6–7, 47
Werbner, Pnina 36
Whitehead, Stephen 18
Wind, Yoram 3
Wood, Julian 26–7, 37

Yates, Maisey 37

For Product Safety Concerns and Information please contact our EU representative GPSR@taylorandfrancis.com
Taylor & Francis Verlag GmbH, Kaufingerstraße 24, 80331 München, Germany

www.ingramcontent.com/pod-product-compliance
Lightning Source LLC
Chambersburg PA
CBHW051800230426
43670CB00012B/2370